Dealing With Difficult People

Practical Techniques For Managing Challenging Relationships

Geoff Marsh

Dansam

Dansam Publishing

Published by Dansam Publishing.

Email: info@dansamltd.co.uk

Web: www.dansamltd.co.uk

For more information about Geoff Marsh and his products/service. email him at geoff@dansamltd.co.uk

ISBN paperback: 978-1-7385517-0-5

ISBN ebook: 978-1-7385517-1-2

Contents

Chapter 1

About The Author

Geoff Marsh is an international trainer, presenter and performance coach. He started his career in 1986 on Lloyds Bank's 'Customer First' Programme. This was one of the largest series of roadshow workshops in the world at the time. The programme was seen by approximately 70,000 staff.

For four decades Geoff has delivered conferences, courses and presentations across the globe.

He started his own company, Dansam Ltd, in 1999. Since then he has delivered courses on a wide variety of subjects, including Dealing With Difficult People for companies such as Robert Bosch Ltd, BNP Paribas, The Wealth Management Institute of Singapore, Barclays, HSBC, and many others.

In addition Geoff is much sought after as a presenter, after-dinner speaker and radio show host.

He is also the author of 'The Insider's Guide to High Performance Presentations' which is available to buy from Amazon.

Chapter 2

Dealing With Difficult People

Let's face it, other people can be annoying.

Whether it is our boss making unreasonable demands, our colleagues not doing their jobs properly, friends letting us down over arrangements we have made, neighbours hosting late night noisy parties, our children's teachers giving excessive homework etc.

Sometimes these things can be minor irritations that pass quickly. Sometimes they can cause much longer-lasting damage and make our lives a misery.

In this book, we delve into the complex dynamics of interacting with individuals whom we commonly label as difficult. We will cover both navigating workplace conflicts and managing challenging personal situations.

Part One: Understanding Foundation Principles

The first part of the book serves as a comprehensive exploration of the foundational principles essential for effectively dealing with difficult people. We begin by examining the underlying reasons why certain individuals exhibit challenging behaviours. We will consider our own perceptions and biases, shedding light on why we categorise others as difficult within our personal and professional spheres.

We delve into the concepts of paradigms and heuristics, uncovering how these cognitive frameworks influence our judgements of others and how others perceive us. By understanding these psychological mechanisms, we can gain insight into the dynamics of interpersonal relationships and learn strategies to navigate them effectively.

We will highlight the need to adopt an assertive approach as a fundamental strategy for dealing with difficult individuals. We define assertiveness and provide practical guidance on how to implement assertive communication techniques in challenging situations. Moreover, we emphasise the importance of using "I" statements as a powerful tool for expressing feelings, needs, and boundaries in conversations with difficult people.

Part Two: Specific Strategies For Different Types Of Difficult People

The second part of the book delves into more specific strategies tailored to address various types of difficult personalities. From **Bullies and Dominators** to **Double-Dealing Deceivers**, **Scornful Snipers**, and **Moaning Monsters**, we offer insights into understanding the behavioural patterns of each archetype. Through practical tips and techniques, we will examine how to effectively manage interactions with these challenging individuals whilst maintaining our composure and self-respect.

Part Three: Addressing Extreme Circumstances

In the third part of the book, we confront the more extreme scenarios where conventional techniques may prove ineffective. We explore situations where individuals exhibit psychopathic or sociopathic tendencies, presenting unique challenges in interpersonal relationships. While these circumstances may be rare, we will consider potential strategies to navigate such encounters with caution and discernment.

What This Book Is About:

Our aim in this book is to provide a toolkit of options to consider when navigating the complexities of dealing with difficult people in various contexts. By understanding the underlying principles, adopting assertive communication techniques, and implementing tailored strategies, we can effectively increase our chances of managing challenging interactions and foster healthier relationships. We hope this book serves as a valuable resource, offering guidance, empowerment and options and to navigate interpersonal conflicts with confidence and resilience.

The intention is that the book covers many realistic situations and may provide a few useful tips and techniques for how you might respond in each case.

What This Book Is NOT About:

While our focus is on providing strategies for navigating challenging interpersonal dynamics, it's important to clarify what this book does not encompass. We acknowledge there are situations that extend beyond the scope of our expertise and may require specialised intervention. Therefore, this book is primarily focused on non-life-threatening scenarios, excluding discussions on physical violence and self-defense. Additionally, we refrain from making judgements on politics or ideologies, recognising that our aim is to offer practical strategies for dealing with difficult individuals irrespective of their beliefs or affiliations.

Our Approach:

At the heart of this book is the recognition that if you perceive someone as difficult, then they are challenging for you, and you seek strategies for managing those interactions. We adopt a reflective approach, urging you to examine your own behaviour and contribution to the dynamics of difficult relationships. By holding up a mirror to our own actions, the aim is to empower us to initiate positive change within ourselves and develop more constructive interactions with others.

We emphasise proactive measures for self-improvement, focusing on how we can modify our behaviour to cultivate more positive and productive relationships. Moreover, we provide specific techniques for responding to the challenging behaviour of others, equipping us with practical tools to navigate difficult situations with confidence and resilience.

Author's Disclaimer:

It's essential to note that the author is not medically or clinically trained, nor a licensed therapist. Rather, the insights and strategies shared in this book are drawn from nearly four decades of experience working with groups and individuals, learning from both successful and challenging interactions. While the advice offered is based on practical wisdom, readers should approach it with the understanding that professional therapeutic intervention may be necessary in certain circumstances. If you feel the need for specialised support, we encourage you to consult a qualified medical practitioner or therapist.

Conclusion:

We trust that the strategies and insights presented in this book will prove valuable in navigating the complexities of dealing with difficult people in various aspects of life. By increasing self-awareness, promoting proactive behaviour change, and offering practical tools for effective communication, we aim to empower readers to navigate challenging interpersonal dynamics with grace and resilience. We hope you find this resource helpful on your journey toward healthier and more fulfilling relationships.

Chapter 3

Why Are Some People Difficult?

Perhaps a better question would be, "Why do we perceive some people as difficult?"

In short, most of us find people 'easy' when they act, think, or behave in a way that matches our expectations of how they should behave.

'Difficult people' on the other hand are people who do not act, think, or behave in a way that matches our expectations.

Does this really make them 'difficult' or just 'different'?

The Map Is Not The Territory

Polish-American scientist and philosopher Alfred Korzybski in 1931 remarked that "the map is not the territory" and that "the word is not the thing".[1]

Imagine a map of Paris. It is a good map. If I were able to show this map to a group of people each would instantly be able to perceive it as Paris.

Of course, it is not Paris. It is just a drawing, a representation, an illustration of Paris. Even the best map of Paris is still just a drawing, an illustration.

Now imagine a truck driver, delivering fish in Paris. (Stay with me, this is going somewhere). The truck driver is lost. The driver uses their mobile phone to speak to the administrator in their company.

"I'm lost." says the driver.

"Relax." says the administrator. "Do you have a map of Paris with you?"

"Yes." says the driver.

"I also have a map." says the administrator. "I can give you some directions."

1. Korzybski, Alfred (1933). International Non-Aristotelian Library Publishing Company.

The administrator takes out their map. It is a beautiful street map of Paris. It contains all the street names, the landmarks, the road numbers and is colour coded.

The driver also has a beautiful map of Paris. But this is the ordinance survey map of Paris. It contains references to the geographical features of the land and the co-ordinates for perfect orienteering.

Both maps are the best money can buy. But imagine the communication between the two people when the administrator says, "You need to drive down the Champs-Elysees."

The driver looks at the ordinance survey map and sees no Champs-Elysees marked on their map. The driver asks, "Is it near a river? Do you have the co-ordinates?"

The communication between these two people will be 'difficult' because, despite having very good quality maps, their maps contain different details.

Each of us face this difficulty with almost everybody with whom we come into contact.

In our heads each of us have a 'map of the world'.

I am not talking about a purely geographical map (though that is there as well). I am talking about an existential 'map'. A 'map' that details to you how the world works.

What is fair and what is unfair? What is moral and immoral? What is right and wrong? What is reasonable and what is unreasonable? What are the rules for success? What is acceptable behaviour in each circumstance?

For each of us, this 'map' has been developing since the day we were born. It is almost impossible to isolate one or two factors that create our personal 'maps of the world'. Everything that happens, everything we experience, adds a little more to our 'map'.

Were you an only child or did you have siblings?

If you had siblings, were you the eldest, youngest or somewhere in the middle?

Were you brought up by both parents? One parent? Neither?

Were your parents or guardians young and healthy when you were born?

We all tend to think we were brought up in the same family as our siblings, but that is not quite true. I was brought up in a family where I was the eldest child. I had a younger brother and a much younger sister. My experience was to be responsible for my siblings, to set a good example, to act my age. When I went to school I was the first of my siblings to do so. I had no older siblings to keep an eye on me and make sure I was OK.

My brother, on the other hand, was born into a family where he had a bossy older brother and an annoying younger sister he used to tease. When my brother started school, he knew I was there in another class. I would keep an eye on him at break time and he even knew some of my friends.

My sister was born into a family where she seemingly had four parents (including two older brothers) all bossing her around and telling her what to do.

It is hardly surprising that our 'maps' are all very different.

Irrespective of your siblings, how was your school experience?

When you went to school did you make friends easily or were you a loner?

Did you adapt well to academic work? or did you prefer sports? Did you find school a form of torture that could not end quick enough?

Every experience you have ever had has added to your 'map of the world'. Your 'map' holds your beliefs, your values, your opinions, your hopes, your fears, your dreams and your aspirations. Your 'map of the world' is your reality of how the world is and has been to you.

But just as our map of Paris is not Paris, it is only an illustration, so our personal 'map of the world' is not the world. It is only our representation of the world. And all our 'maps' are different.

As the driver and the administrator will face difficulties in communicating with each other when giving directions, because their maps contain different details, so you and I may have difficulty communicating when I am trying to convey my thoughts using my 'map of the world' and you are trying to understand me using yours. Our 'maps' will differ in millions of ways and each of those differences could cause us to perceive each other as difficult.

For example:

Navigating Expectations: Punctuality In The Workplace

Punctuality at work is a common source of contention, often stemming from differing interpretations of what it means to be "on time." Let's explore this scenario through the lens of conflicting perspectives and personal experiences.

The Contract Conundrum:

Consider a scenario where an employee's contract stipulates working hours from 8:30 a.m. to 5:00 p.m. However, ambiguity arises regarding whether an 8:30 a.m. start entails "arriving at the office at 8:30 a.m." or "being in place and ready to start work at 8:30 a.m."

Manager's Expectations:

From the manager's perspective, punctuality extends beyond mere arrival time; it entails being seated at one's desk and fully prepared to commence work precisely at 8:30 a.m. This perspective is rooted in a belief that punctuality reflects professionalism and dedication to one's role.

Personal Maps And Influences:

Individual perceptions of punctuality are shaped by personal experiences and upbringing. Some employees, and perhaps the manager, adhere to a strict interpretation of punctuality instilled in childhood. For example, a sense of duty and responsibility cultivated by parents or reinforced by school rules may influence the belief that one should always be in place and ready to start work at the designated time.

External Influences:

External factors, such as experiences in previous workplaces, can also shape one's approach to punctuality. If an employee had, in a previous company, demonstrated loyalty and exceeded expectations, only to be made redundant, they may now adopt a more rigid adherence to contractual terms as a form of self-protection. In this case, the employee may adhere strictly to the contract's stated start time without going above and beyond expectations.

Unless the contract specifically defines that an 8.30 a.m. start means 'being in your place of work and ready to start operating by 8.30 a.m.' this is open to interpretation.

Consequently, both the manager and the employee can defend their positions according to their 'map of the world'

So how could this conflict ever be resolved?

Navigating Differences:

In navigating these differing perspectives, communication and mutual understanding are key. Employees and managers alike must recognise and respect each other's interpretations of punctuality. Open dialogue can help clarify expectations and develop a collaborative approach to time management in the workplace.

In other words, they will need to talk to each other.

Who Is Right?

The answer depends on your 'map of the world'.

Punctuality in the workplace is not simply a matter of showing up on time; it encompasses a range of interpretations shaped by personal experiences, cultural norms, and professional expectations. By acknowledging and understanding these differences, individuals can work together to cultivate a workplace culture that values punctuality whilst respecting individual needs and perspectives.

The manager may be ambitious and has recognised that punctuality and preparedness has led to promotion and success. With these details on the manager's 'map', it is hardly surprising that the manager expects their team to hold the same values.

The employee, on the other hand, having been made redundant from a previous job after years of loyal service has a 'map of the world' that now says, "Do only what is required. Your extra efforts are neither appreciated nor rewarded."

When it comes to dealing with difficult people, we need to be aware of our 'map of the world' and that of the other person.

Is the person really difficult or are they just seeing the world/event/situation/problem differently from you?

There are two statements about human beings that are arguably universal.

The first statement is easy to accept:

'Everyone is different.'

Most of us do not have a problem with this. We accept we are all unique and different and see the world in different ways.

The second statement is this:

'Those differences make us respond differently to the same situations.'

This one is much harder to process but is equally true.

Whenever you find yourself thinking:

"But it's obvious, why can't they see it?"

"Why are they being so unreasonable?"

"Why don't they reach the same conclusion as me?"

The answer is that they are different from you. Their 'map of the world' is different from yours.

It is obvious to you because your 'map' contains information that helps you reach that conclusion. This information may be your education, your life experience, your physical health, your family background, the books you have read, or the TV programmes you have seen.

To someone who has not had your education, or your life experience, or your physical health, or your family background, or read the same books as you, the conclusion may be far from obvious.

Some of the things we take for granted as absolute 'truths' may not be the same for everybody.

I was once having dinner with a close friend. I am from the UK. He is from the USA. Our meal was served, and I watched as he cut up all his food into bite-sized chunks. Then he put down his knife and ate only with his fork.

I laughed at him and said, "If my mother saw you doing that she would ask if you were a baby who was so afraid of choking that you needed to cut up your food into tiny pieces?"

He laughed and looked at me holding my knife and fork and said, "If my mother saw you holding both your knife and fork through the entire meal she might ask what's the matter? Can't you shovel it in fast enough?"

We are good friends and laughed together at the different subconscious beliefs we both held, even with something as simple as eating a meal.

But imagine that instead of something as trivial as holding your knife and fork, this were a deeply held political or religious view, it would be easy to see how this could become a difficult situation.

We never really know someone else's 'map of the world'. We don't live their lives.

When dealing with 'difficult' people it is vital to remember this.

- Most people do not wake up in the same house as you.
- They don't have the same breakfast as you.
- They don't enjoy the same relationships as you.
- They don't have the same journey to work as you.

Some people face imaginable challenges just to get themselves to school or work each morning.

A friend was complaining about an acquaintance. He had met her on the street and said afterwards how cold she was towards him and how much older she looked since the last time he had seen her. He was then informed that the poor lady's son had died recently. Suddenly the coldness and the ageing made sense.

We do not know what horrors and challenges others are facing.

Your 'map of the world' may be of a place of peace. Theirs may be a war zone.

Paradigms And Heuristics

Many years ago, I came across the subject of 'Paradigms' when I read 'Paradigms – Discovering the Future by Joel Barker.[2]

Paradigms may be defined as deeply ingrained mental models or patterns of thought that dictate how we perceive reality, interpret information, and make sense of our experiences. These paradigms act as lenses through which we filter and process incoming stimuli, guiding our actions and shaping our responses to various situations.

A paradigm is a mathematical concept. It gives us a shortcut to understanding certain mathematical terms. Shapes, for example, are paradigms.

If I say the word 'triangle' you will instantly have an idea of a three-sided shape.

If I say 'square' you will know I am referring to something with four equal sides.

A paradigm, in that sense, defines the edges, the parameters, the borders.

In business, a paradigm is 'the way we usually do it'.

Our habits, procedures, routines, traditions, and policies are all examples of paradigms. They are shortcuts to

2. Paradigms: The Business of Discovering the Future by Joel A. Barker. Harper Business

helping us recognise how to arrive at a solution more quickly.

A simple example of this is tying your shoelaces.

We normally learn to tie our shoelaces somewhere between the ages of 4 and 8 years old. Today you may be in your 30s or 40s, but you probably still tie your shoelaces in the same way you did when you were between the ages of 4 and 8 years old.

It is unlikely you wake up every morning and ask, "How am I going to tie my shoelaces today?" You haven't got time for that, and you have more important things to worry about, so you rely on your shoelace-tying paradigm as a time-saving autopilot that leaves you free to concentrate on more important issues.

Paradigms save us time by preventing us from having to reinvent the wheel every time we do an activity.

Imagine how much time we would lose if we had to re-learn everything every day.

The problem with paradigms comes when we start to believe that our way of doing a task, our paradigm, is not just the best paradigm we currently have, but is the *only* paradigm.

Barker describes this as 'paradigm paralysis'.

The human brain is very good at processing some information, but not so good at processing other information.

Information The Brain Processes Well:

- Information we like
- Information with which we agree
- Information that supports our argument
- Information we have come across previously
- Information we expected to hear or see

The brain processes all this information at a lightning speed.

On the other hand

Information The Brain Does Not Process Well:

- Information with which we disagree
- Information we don't like
- Information that is counter to our argument
- Information we have not experienced previously
- Information that is different from what we expected

The brain really struggles to process this information.

For example.

Answer this question:

How many animals of each species did Moses take on the ark?

If your brain answered '2' to this question, then read it again.

Most people answer '2' to this question. This is the case whether the question is asked verbally or in written form as it is here.

The real answer is 'zero'. Moses didn't take any animals onto the ark. It was Noah's ark.

Logically this should be obvious to everybody. I have asked this question across the globe and the majority, no matter what their religion, have some awareness of the story of Noah's ark.

It should, therefore, be obvious that Moses did not go on the ark and took no animals with him. So why is it so hard to see?

The answer is...paradigms.

Some of the information in this question fits our expectations. Many of us were taught when were small children that the animals went onto the ark 'two by two'.

We see the part of the question that says 'how many animals....went onto the ark' and we know the answer is '2'. The question also contains one piece of information that does not fit and should not be there i.e. 'Moses'

What does our brain do with this piece of information? It deletes it and pretends it does not exist.

This is OK for a silly question like the one above but how does this work in real life?

I once met my wife from the railway station. It was a surprise. I was supposed to be at work, but I finished early and thought it would be a nice idea if I picked her up from the station instead of leaving her to get a taxi.

The station only had one exit. I was standing at one end of the tunnel and saw my wife approaching. I looked at her and she looked back with no sense of recognition. When she drew level with me, she walked straight past.

I went after her and tapped her on the shoulder and she jumped in shock. She gave me a look that I can only describe as, "Who are you?"

This lasted just a few seconds, and then she smiled in recognition as her brain registered it was me.

To her credit she said later, "I thought you looked familiar." After nearly 40 years of being together you would hope that I did!

So what happened here?

My wife's paradigm was that I was at work. I could not be there to pick her up from the station. Even when her eyes gave her information that contradicted this belief, she chose to go with the belief that it couldn't be me.

Someone who has worked inside a company for a long time has developed lots of company-specific paradigms. Over the years they have been with the company they have encountered lots of problems and crises. Through trial and error, through following (or not following) procedure and through bitter experience, they have learned how to get through these problems and crises as painlessly as possible.

When they encounter a particular problem, their brain sifts back through their memory to find a time when they last had this particular problem. The brain asks, "How did we resolve that problem last time?" and then proceeds to apply the same solution to the current problem. In other words, we now have a paradigm for solving this particular problem – the way we usually solve this.

But imagine someone new joining the team. This newcomer previously worked for a competitor company. In this competitor company they did things very differently. The newcomer has different paradigms they like to apply to problems and crises.

In both cases the team members know their own problem-solving paradigms have worked. If each of their previous paradigms had not worked, they would have abandoned them in favour of those that did.

So, each employee has faith and belief that their way works. They can support that belief with practical evidence of past success. Now they are faced with someone trying to do it a different way.

It is likely each would perceive the other as 'difficult'.

Barker encourages us to cultivate a mindset of curiosity and openness, challenging conventional wisdom and questioning established norms. By recognising the influence of paradigms on our perceptions and behaviours, individuals can break free from limiting beliefs and embrace the potential for growth, innovation, and transformation in both personal and professional spheres.

A similar concept to 'paradigms' is that of heuristics.

In his amazing book, Thinking, Fast and Slow,[3] Daniel Kahneman describes heuristics as mental shortcuts or rules of thumb that individuals use to make quick decisions and solve problems efficiently, often in situations where exhaustive analysis or perfect information is not feasible. These cognitive shortcuts allow people to streamline complex decision-making processes by relying on simplified strategies or generalisations based on past experiences, intuition, or commonly held beliefs. While heuristics can be valuable tools for rapid decision-making, they can also lead to biases and errors in judgement, as they may overlook important information or fail to account for situational nuances. Despite their limitations, heuristics play a fundamental role in human cognition, enabling individuals to navigate uncertainty and make decisions effectively in a wide range of contexts.

In the book Kahneman describes several key heuristics such as:

The Anchoring Heuristic

With this heuristic we are more likely to be influenced by the first piece of information learned when making a choice. This influence can persist even if it is not particularly relevant to the situation in question.

---

3. Thinking, Fast and Slow: by Daniel Kahneman, Penguin Publishers

This might be why many people vote for the same political parties as their parents or support the same football team. If you were taken to watch a football match as a child by a family member and you stood with supporters of a particular team and participated in the jubilant celebrations of that team winning, it is likely to have the effect of engendering a lifetime of support for that team.

Nationalism might be described as an effect of the anchoring heuristic. We each found ourselves citizens of a particular country as an accident of birth. I didn't choose to be born in the UK. It was a combination of factors outside my control. It is illogical, therefore, to have a greater pride in 'my' country than any other. Nevertheless, that is what many of us do.

My youngest daughter moved in with her boyfriend. As they faced their first Christmas together, they faced the dilemma of what Christmas tree to buy – Real or artificial?

My daughter argued strongly for a fake Christmas tree. Cheaper, less messy, reusable and easier to find one to match the available space in their living room.

All logical arguments.

Her boyfriend on the other hand argued, equally strongly, for a real Christmas tree. More environmentally friendly, they look better, and provide a great talking point for visitors. These were also logical arguments.

As a parent, I wonder how much of their argument was governed by the fact that my wife and I have always had artificial trees whilst her boyfriend's parents had always had real trees.

Was this the anchoring heuristic in action? Each of them 'anchored' by their experiences of Christmas with their own families.

I have delivered training on negotiation skills for more than 20 years and have seen the 'anchoring' effect in action many times.

The final outcome of many negotiations was often determined by the starting points of each party.

Imagine Sarah wants to sell an object for £150. When preparing for the negotiation she realises that if she starts the negotiation by asking for £150, she is likely to be 'beaten down' and achieve less than £150. Therefore, she intends to start the negotiation by asking for £200.

The negotiation begins and Helen, the buyer, makes an opening offer of £50.

Sarah panics. How can she possibly ask for £200 when Helen has only offered £50? This low 'anchoring' price of £50 suddenly frames the whole negotiation. Sarah may counter with £150 or (in my observed experience) even less.

The £200 opening offer, that Sarah had prepared, disappears, and is never mentioned or discussed. The opening 'anchoring' price of £50 has had a huge psychological effect on Sarah's confidence. This is highly illogical. Helen might never have expected Sarah to accept such a low offer but she wanted to 'test the water' to see

Sarah's reaction to £50. Had Sarah ignored the anchor and countered with £200 the final price would likely to have been higher for Sarah. The anchoring heuristic can be a powerful determinant.

In both examples given here, the 'difficult situation' has been created and made worse by the anchoring heuristic. The argument over Christmas trees was largely caused by the initial 'priming' of both partners. Both had their starting positions determined by their parent's choices.

In the negotiation example Sarah's job is made harder by being influenced by the 'anchoring' and 'priming' from Helen.

The Availability Heuristic

This is the process of judging frequency and probability by how easy it is to think of an example. This can lead to some strongly held views about whether or not something has happened, can happen or is likely to happen in the future.

If you have been involved in a road accident yourself or know someone who has been injured in a road accident you are more likely to be worried about speeding motorists than someone who has never been affected by such incidents.

Someone who has been the victim of cyber-crime or identity theft is much more likely to be concerned about internet security than someone who has not.

This is, of course, fairly obvious.

The problem comes in a discussion between two people when either party is unaware of the availability heuristic the other is using.

Brexit was a hugely divisive issue in the UK and the availability heuristic may have played a large part in the way many voted.

I once saw an argument between two friends who were on opposite sides of the argument. The debate got heated because neither side could appreciate the position of the other.

As an objective observer it was easier for me to listen to the points they were making. One of them lived in the northeast of the UK and came from Grimsby. Grimsby was once the largest fishing port in Europe. On joining the EEC, fishing quotas were agreed and it appeared to many fishing families in Grimsby that their livelihoods had been decimated by joining the EEC. Today Grimsby is regarded as one of the most deprived areas in the UK. For some of the residents here, their availability heuristic told them that being a member of the EU had led directly to job losses in their area. All the news reports and proclamations from politicians and celebrities would not change that belief.

"I don't care what they say on the news. All I know is it happened here." might be the cry.

My other friend was born in the UK and had married a French man. Her sons were both half-French. Her stepson was French and lived in France. From her perspective, Brexit had divided her family and split the UK from France. Her emotional pain was visceral and her fear of the consequences of the UK decision to leave the EU was real and undeniable.

“My family are not French or British, they are European, and those Brexit fools don’t seem to care.” might be the cry here.

Any rational discussion on the socio-political and economic effects of Brexit were filtered (for both of them) through this availability heuristic.

Both saw the other as ‘difficult’ and it is not hard to see why.

The Covid-19 pandemic also led to divisions from those who believe it is the worst health crisis the world has faced since the Spanish Flu outbreak in 1918. Others believe it was massively overblown and that the over-reaction had more to do with political expediency than health imperatives.

Once again, the availability heuristic is likely to have played a part here.

For people who experienced bad cases of Covid themselves, lost loved ones or saw Covid devastate the long-term health of friends and family, the measures could hardly have been strict enough. Anyone who doubted the seriousness of Covid was a Covid-denier and a fool.

For people who did not have Covid themselves or who had never seen friends, family or even acquaintances affected after more than two years of the disease, the lockdown of the global economy and the various restrictions on freedom and liberty could seem quite sinister.

Both may listen to data, information and statistics that supports their position, whilst ridiculing the position of the other.

Brexit and Covid are highly-emotive and extreme examples of the availability heuristic we observe around us all the time at work and at home.

I was once called into a department to help the sales team. The manager of the team explained the sales team were not achieving their targets and had a very low level of profitability. When I spoke to the team, they explained away their poor sales and low profitability due to the fact that, "We are just too expensive." They firmly believed that their product was over-priced. When I asked them why they thought this, they answered, "All our customers tell us we are over-priced and they can get our product cheaper elsewhere."

On investigation and research, we quickly discovered through competitor benchmarking that not only was this department NOT the most expensive, they were (by a factor of five in some cases) the cheapest in the market.

When this information was fed back to the team, they were highly sceptical. After all, why would their customers lie?

But their customers were lying. It is in the interest of customers to say the price is too high in the hope you will lower it. This is what had happened with the department in question. When we investigated further, we could only uncover a couple of stories where customers had complained about the price. Unfortunately, these few instances were shared and shared until they became the absolute truth for all clients.

Because everybody could instantly think of examples of where clients had complained about the price it became a reality for all clients. This is the availability heuristic in action.

With all the examples I have quoted, here, (especially Brexit and Covid) you might find yourself asking, "But what about the truth? Surely the facts should speak for themselves." You may even be able to present whole reports of 'facts' but the heuristics can be powerful determinants of an individual's belief. Even in the face of overwhelming evidence to the contrary it can be difficult for people to change that belief. The availability heuristic is a strong force.

So Why Are People Difficult?

We return to the question posed at the beginning of this chapter. Why do we *perceive* some people as difficult?

We are governed by our paradigms and heuristics which make up our 'map of the world'. These paradigms and heuristics affect the way we process the information and stimuli we encounter. If the information presented fits with our paradigms and is in accordance with our heuristics, we find it easy to process. If the information presented does not fit our paradigms or is not in accordance with our heuristics we find it difficult to process. It is easy to reach the conclusion that if someone is presenting information that is 'difficult' to process they must be a 'difficult' person.

We must also keep in mind that, whilst the other person is governed by their paradigms and heuristics, so are we. To them we may appear 'difficult'.

Chapter 4

How To Deal With Difficult People

The Starting point?

When encountering 'difficult' people or dealing with 'difficult' situations it is worth remembering the adage:

To be understood, first seek to understand

This has been attributed to many people over the years. The first instance I could find of this being attributed to anyone was St Francis of Assisi. And who are we to argue with St Francis?

It's a powerful statement.

If you want to change someone's mind, how can you change their mind until you know where their mind is?

The statement "To be understood, first seek to understand" is a foundational principle of effective communication and interpersonal relationships, particularly when dealing with difficult people. By embodying this mindset, individuals can shift their focus from defending their own perspectives or seeking validation, to genuinely listening to and empathising with the perspectives and experiences of others.

When applied to interactions with difficult people, this principle serves several purposes:

Facilitating Empathy:

Empathy is possibly an overused term. Sometimes we use it without thinking about what it really means. According to Wikipedia, 'Empathy is generally described as the ability to take on another's perspective, to understand, feel and possibly share and respond to their experience.' The ability to 'share' the feelings of another is easier to say than it is to do. It is the ultimate expression of what it means to truly try to understand another person's 'map of the world'.

There is an old expression that says "You can never truly know another person until you have walked a mile in their shoes." This can be taken literally as well as metaphorically.

Imagine actually walking a mile in another person's shoes. You might discover the shoes are uncomfortable or that they have a stone in them. You might discover the person walks in a place where the temperature is icy cold or that their home lies within a war zone. Literally walking a mile in their shoes might reveal much about their 'map of the world' and how it affects the way they respond to any given situation.

But it is probably more practical to imagine it in a metaphorical sense. Imagine yourself in their world. If you were facing some of the challenges facing the other person, how might you respond?

Seeking to understand the motivations, concerns, and emotions of difficult individuals builds empathy and compassion, which can help defuse tensions and build rapport. By empathising with their perspective, individuals can demonstrate they value and respect the other person's feelings and experiences, even if they disagree with their behaviour.

Promoting Active Listening:

Actively listening to the concerns and perspectives of difficult people demonstrates genuine interest and engagement in their point of view. This not only validates their feelings but also encourages open and honest communication, creating a conducive environment for constructive dialogue and problem-solving.

Identifying Root Causes:

Understanding the underlying reasons behind the difficult behaviour can provide valuable insights into the root causes of the conflict or tension. By delving beneath the surface and exploring the motivations and triggers driving the other person's actions, individuals can uncover common ground and identify potential solutions to address the underlying issues.

Building Trust And Respect:

Demonstrating a sincere effort to understand the perspectives of difficult individuals can help build trust and respect in the relationship. When people feel heard and understood, they are more likely to reciprocate by listening to, and considering alternative viewpoints, thereby developing mutual understanding and cooperation.

Promoting Collaboration:

By prioritising understanding over judgement or criticism, individuals can create a collaborative atmosphere where both parties feel valued and respected. This collaborative approach encourages brainstorming, compromise, and consensus-building, leading to more effective conflict resolution and positive outcomes for all involved.

In essence, the principle of "To be understood, first seek to understand" stresses the importance of empathy, active listening, and genuine curiosity in navigating challenging interpersonal dynamics. By embracing this mindset, individuals can transform conflicts into opportunities for growth, connection, and mutual understanding, even in interactions with the most difficult of people.

Understanding another person's internal 'map of the world', including their paradigms and heuristics, can significantly enhance the effectiveness of your communication and argumentation.

Here are some examples of how this understanding can be leveraged to position your arguments in a way the other person is more likely to accept:

Tailoring Communication Style:

If you understand the other person tends to favour concrete examples and practical applications over abstract theories, you can frame your arguments using real-life scenarios and tangible outcomes. By aligning your communication style with their preferred mode of processing information, you increase the likelihood they will engage with and accept your arguments.

Addressing Core Beliefs:

By delving into the other person's paradigms and deeply held beliefs, you can identify common ground or shared values that can serve as a basis for your argument. For example, if you know they prioritise fairness and equality, you can frame your argument in terms of how your proposal aligns with these values, making it more palatable and convincing to them.

Anticipating Biases And Preconceptions:

Understanding the heuristics and biases that influence the other person's decision-making can help you anticipate potential objections or counterarguments. By pre-emptively addressing these concerns and reframing your arguments to mitigate bias, you increase the likelihood of them accepting your perspective.

Appealing To Emotional Resonance:

People are often more receptive to arguments that resonate with their emotional experiences or personal narratives. By tapping into the other person's emotional landscape and leveraging stories or anecdotes that align with their lived experiences, you can create a deeper emotional connection.

Offering Incremental Change:

If the other person's paradigms or heuristics predispose them to resist radical change or disruption, you can position your arguments in a way that emphasises gradual progress or incremental improvements. By framing your proposal as a natural extension of existing practices or as a logical next step in their established worldview, you reduce resistance and increase receptivity to your ideas.

By understanding and empathising with the other person's internal 'map of the world', including their paradigms and heuristics, you can tailor your arguments to resonate more effectively with their mindset and perspective. This approach not only increases the likelihood of them accepting your arguments but also develops a deeper understanding and connection in the communication process.

Chapter 5

Assertiveness

Assertive behaviour is extremely useful when dealing with difficult people. But what does it mean to be assertive?

The best way to understand assertiveness is to compare and contrast it with aggressive and submissive behaviour.

Submissive People:

Being submissive means giving up your own needs in favour of others, even when you don't need to, or it is not in your own best interests.

Submissive People:

- Want to be liked
- Don't like to disappoint or upset others
- Give way when it is not in their own best interests
- Fear sticking up for themselves or putting forward their own view
- Try to accommodate everybody's needs except their

own

- Feel like victims
- Seem to pursue a lose-win strategy (the submissive person loses whilst everyone around them wins)
- Avoid conflict
- Make concessions in the hope the other person will like them (or take pity on them) and give something back in return
- Try to kill their enemies with kindness

Aggressive People:

Being aggressive means putting your needs and interests above all others, even when you don't need to, or it works against your own best interests.

Aggressive People:

- Want to be respected or feared
- Recognise you cannot keep everybody happy and there is no point in trying. After all, you can't make an omelette without breaking some eggs
- Demand others give way or face the consequences
- Put their own needs above others at all times
- Welcome conflict
- Demand concessions from others as the price for maintaining the relationship

- Pursue a win-lose strategy (the aggressive person wins whilst those around lose)
- Consider kindness as a weakness to be exploited

Assertive People:

- Treat people with respect
- Consider most situations as problems to be solved (it's not only about winning)
- Work to be firm but fair
- Stand up for their own needs and rights whilst respecting and accommodating the needs of others as much as possible
- Pursue a win-win strategy
- Try to find a solution that meets of many of their needs and as many of the needs of the other side as possible

Nobody is assertive all the time. We all behave aggressively and submissively at times.

Parents, for example, will sometimes behave submissively with their children as a way of letting them learn. Many parents recognise that sometimes you have to let children win an argument or a game in order for them to build their self-confidence.

When we are in physical danger or in crisis, we may behave aggressively to prevent ourselves or those we love from being hurt or damaged.

If you saw somebody physically attacking a family member or friend you may decide this is not the best time to try and 'reason' with the attacker. You may aggressively stop the attack and afterwards try to work out what happened.

The Essence Of Assertiveness

Assertiveness means being clear about your 'personal rights'. These are not all legal rights. They do not ignore your responsibilities. They are, instead, a series of beliefs that define assertive people.

When I was young my father taught me a valuable life lesson when he said, "Nobody is better than you."

I was puzzled. I said, "But some people are taller than I am, richer than I am, better looking. Some people can play football better than me, ride a bike better than me, live in a bigger house than me. Some people have a better education than me."

My father smiled and said, "That just makes them different from you. It doesn't make them better."

It was a valuable life lesson lesson and one I still hold dear to my heart.

I have met many wealthy people in my life. Some got there by hard work. Some got there through luck, and some inherited their wealth. Despite their wealth, I have frequently observed how many of them have had marital problems or problems with their children. Issues related to drugs, alcohol and gambling are also common problems. Just because people are wealthy, doesn't mean they have all the answers.

I have met people who have been to better schools, achieved higher grades or even gone on to the highest levels of education available. In discussions, however, I have often observed a staggering lack of common sense.

I worked with an extremely intelligent engineer. We were working on a project together and we had to price the job to our client. I was working on one part of the proposal. He was working on how many people the job would need.

He proudly presented his figures to me and said, "This job can be done in three weeks with two and a half people."

I looked at him, puzzled. "Two and a half people?" I asked.

"Yes," he said confidently, "I have broken down the job into modules. Calculated how long (in hours) it will take to complete each module and in order to meet the deadline of three weeks it will take two and a half people working eight hours per day."

He looked so proud of his calculation I felt really bad asking him, "Where are we going to find half a person?"

He looked confused. His calculations were faultless. It had not occurred to him that there was no such thing as half a person. You can have one person working for four hours but you cannot have half a person working for eight hours.

Better educated than me? Definitely. But did this make him better than me in every way?

I should not, however, forget the second part of my father's advice.

He did say "Nobody is better than you, they are just different." Then he also added "But that doesn't make you better than them, just different."

It's a good philosophy and one I have held dearly whether I am working with interns or CEOs, sewage workers or royalty.

Underpinning this belief are some important personal rights. These are beliefs, as opposed to actual legal rights.

Here are some of the personal rights that form the beliefs of assertive people:

1. I Have A Right To Make Mistakes

This does not mean you have an obligation to make mistakes. It does not mean you will aim to make mistakes. It does mean that, as a member of the human race, you will make mistakes whether you want to or not. Nobody likes to make a mistake. But if you do make a mistake, you will not beat yourself up for the rest of eternity. You will take whatever steps you can to avoid making that mistake again but you will forgive yourself. Human beings make mistakes and you are human being.

2. I Have A Right To My Own Opinions And Views

This does not mean you are entitled to force your views on others but as a human being you will have your own thoughts, feelings, views, and opinions whether you want to or not. Assertive people believe their opinions and views are just as valid as those of anyone else. Aim to furnish yourself with as much evidence as you can to back up your opinions and views and be prepared to listen to the views and opinions as others but do not give them more weight than you should. Even children have opinions and sometimes they are better than the views and opinions of the adults around them.

3. I Have The Right To Change My Mind

As the facts or the situation changes you may find a decision or choice you made previously no longer applies. Submissive people are afraid to change their mind in case they are attacked or criticised for being weak or indecisive. Assertive people recognise that changing our mind is sometimes the wisest course of action. Sometimes your feelings will change and this may affect your decision. Yesterday I felt like eating crumpets or going for a walk. Today I don't feel like eating crumpets or going for a walk. I have changed my mind. It's OK to do that.

4. I Have A Right To Ignore The Advice Of Others

Everybody has an opinion, and they are entitled to have that opinion. They are not entitled to foist it on others. Assertive people will listen to the advice but feel no obligation to act upon it or take it into themselves. Nobody else lives your life. Most people give advice based upon what *they* would do in your situation. But they are not you. They do not share your 'map of the world' and, most importantly, they do not have to live with the consequences of you following their advice. If it all goes wrong they will say to you, "Well I only offered a suggestion, you didn't have to follow it." It is worth remembering that *before* you follow their advice, rather than afterwards.

5. I Have A Right To Say 'NO'

Clearly this is not always the case. You do not normally have a right to say "no" to tax demands, to following the law or following health and safety guidelines. This right refers to the times when there is no legal or health and safety imperative e.g. requests from friends, family. colleagues or even your boss.

We are not talking about your boss saying, "You are contractually obligated to fulfill this deadline and you cannot say no."

We are talking about when your boss asks you to cover for a colleague who is off work, or asks you to work overtime when you already have plans of your own. If these are genuine requests (not polite commands) then you do have the right to say "no". If a friend asks you take care of their cat whilst they are away for a few days, and you know you are extremely busy all weekend you have the right to say "no". Why are your plans less important than those of your friend? If a family member asks you to take them to the airport early on a Saturday morning and you have been working extremely hard all week and desperately need the weekend to recuperate, it is OK to say "no". Your need is as great as theirs. Yes, it will make their life harder if you say "no". But if you say "yes" it will make your life harder. Why should their needs take precedence over yours? You may not always choose to exercise this right to say "no" but be aware it is your right. This took me many years to learn. As a people pleaser it was tempting to make people happy with me by agreeing to demands that made me unhappy. My people pleasing seemed to include everybody except me. Eventually I started to ask myself, "If I asked a friend or family member to take me to the airport on a Saturday morning, and they replied they couldn't do it because they were busy or had just finished a long week, how would I feel?" The answer is that it would be inconvenient for me, but I would understand and make alternative arrangements. I may also think twice at a later date if they asked me for a favour, but this fact alone does not oblige me to say "yes" every time.

6. I Have A Right Not To Have To Justify Myself To Others

This is one of the most important assertive rights. Submissive people feel the need to justify their actions to others and if they cannot provide a sufficient justification then they must submit to the needs of others. Assertive people do not accept this. We are not in a court of law. There is no duty to provide empirical evidence for your feelings.

If you say to your host, “I am sorry I don’t like prunes.” and your host says, “Why not?” how is this question going to help anybody?

If you cannot come up with a good reason why you don’t like prunes, does that mean your host can start shovelling prunes onto your plate and expect you to eat them? Surely it is enough that you don’t like them.

If you are invited to the theatre and you say, “No thanks I don’t want to go.” how is it going to help when you are asked, “But why don’t you want to go?”

If you give an answer such as, “I am washing my hair that night.” it is likely to be countered with, “Can’t you wash your hair another night?” This might go on until you can’t think of a good reason why you don’t want to go to the theatre and the other person has won. The consequence is that you will go to the theatre against your will and probably have a miserable evening. Assertive people recognise that it is enough they don’t want to go. They do not have to explain or justify themselves to others. They may justify themselves if they wish, but they have a right not to do so.

7. I Have A Right Not To Anticipate The Needs And Wishes Of Others

Submissive people often face the criticism from others along the lines of "Didn't you think about how that would make me feel?" or "It was inconsiderate of you not to take my feelings into account." Assertive people are not unfeeling or inconsiderate, but they do not accept they must consider EVERYBODY's feelings when making a decision. We cannot keep everyone happy all the time and it is not our responsibility to do that. You might want to spend the evening at home reading a book when your friend had hoped you were going to join them at the pub. The fact that your friend wanted an evening at the pub is not more important than your wish to read the book. You are not living for them. You are living for you.

Have a look at the following situations.

Can you identify if the response is assertive, aggressive or submissive?

Situation 1

A client meets with you and immediately asks you to reduce your costs to match your competitors. He says, "Is that OK for you then?"

Response

"Well, I need to talk to my boss but that should be OK."

Is the response assertive, aggressive or submissive?

Situation 2

Your assistant interrupts you during an important phone call. Your assistant says that one of your difficult clients is on the telephone demanding to talk to you immediately.

Response

"Please explain that I have to finish this call, then I'd be happy to have a word with him. Ask him to leave me a number where I can call him or ask him to call back in 15 minutes if not."

Is the response assertive, aggressive or submissive?

Situation 3

Your colleague has not provided you with the information you requested.

Response

"You're being unreasonable! There's no way we can proceed without these details."

Is the response assertive, aggressive or submissive?

Situation 4

A client was supposed to pay your invoice this week. The payment has not been made.

Response

"I understand you were going to transfer those funds into the account. Has something happened?"

Is the response assertive, aggressive or submissive?

Situation 5

Your brother is complaining that he called during the night, and you were not available. It was most inconvenient because he wanted your advice.

Response

"I am concerned that you were unhappy, but when you expect me to be available 24 hours a day I feel under enormous pressure. I will always try to be available but there are times when it will be unavoidable for me to be unavailable."

Is the response assertive, aggressive or submissive?

The Answers:

Situation 1

A client meets with you and immediately asks you to reduce your costs to match your competitors. He says, "Is that OK for you then?"

Response

"Well, I need to talk to my boss but that should be OK."

Answer:

This is submissive. The client gave you the opportunity to push back when they said, "Is that OK for you then?"

You may feel that you have not agreed to this request by saying "I need to talk to my boss."

Unfortunately, by adding "...but that should be OK" there is only one part of that sentence the client will remember i.e. "That should be OK."

If your boss does say "no" and you return to your client with this answer, the client is likely to counter, "But you said it should be OK." and conflict will ensue.

Had you replied, "I need to discuss this with my boss, and I will get back to you." that would have been an assertive response.

Situation 2

Your assistant interrupts you during an important phone call. Your assistant says that one of your difficult clients is on the telephone demanding to talk to you immediately.

Response

"Please explain that I must finish this call, then I'd be happy to have a word with him. Ask him to leave me a number where I can call him or ask him to call back in 15 minutes if not."

Answer:

This is assertive.

This is a good illustration of being firm but fair.

It is an important telephone call. It would be submissive to hang up because of the interruption. It would be aggressive to dismiss the client because you are busy.

By explaining that you are in the middle of something, but you will be happy to speak afterwards and offering the client an alternative, you are treating your client, your telephone call, and yourself with respect and courtesy.

Situation 3

Your colleague has not provided you with the information you requested.

Response

"You're being unreasonable! There's no way we can proceed without these details."

Answer:

This is aggressive.

It may be the case that your colleague is behaving badly in not providing the information you requested but by saying "you're being unreasonable" you have made a judgement on that colleague. Nobody likes to be called 'unreasonable'. Everybody sees their own behaviour as reasonable. It is likely that your colleague has a reason for not providing the information. By making an accusation it may cause your colleague to become more hostile to your request and cause further delays.

Had you omitted "you're being unreasonable" and simply said, "There is no way we can proceed without these details" you have made a statement of fact. Your colleague, no longer feeling attacked, may explain why the details have not been provided and you may be able to work together to find a solution more quickly.

If your colleague is being deliberately obstructive, you have made your statement clearly and if there are consequences to the information not being provided, your colleague cannot protest they did not know the information was needed.

Any blame for the consequences now falls on your colleague's shoulders.

Situation 4

A client was supposed to pay your invoice this week. The payment has not been made.

Response

"I understand you were going to transfer those funds into the account. Has something happened?"

Answer:

This is assertive.

This time you are not attacking or making any accusations.

You have explained your expectations and requested an explanation as to why those expectations were not met.

Situation 5

Your brother is complaining that he called during the night, and you were not available. It was most inconvenient because he wanted your advice.

Response

"I am concerned that you were unhappy, but when you expect me to be available 24 hours a day I feel under enormous pressure. I will always try to be available but there are times when it will be unavoidable for me to be unavailable."

Answer:

This is assertive.

The respondent treats the brother with respect, whilst maintaining their own right to be unavailable at times.

The main area on which to concentrate here are sentences such as:

"I am concerned that you were unhappy."

"I feel under enormous pressure."

"I will always try to be available."

These are known as 'I' statements and are indispensable when to comes to dealing with difficult people.

Chapter 6

Introducing 'I' Statements

In the dim and distant past when I used to have hair, my hair was red. I certainly matched the stereotype of a 'fiery' redhead. I still have a quick temper, but as a young man my mother would say, "You could start a fight in an empty room."

I wish I had known about 'I' statements when I was younger. I believe they would have saved me a lot of trouble.

Of all the techniques for dealing with difficult people, 'I' statements are among the most powerful.

One of the personal rights noted earlier was 'I have a right to my own opinions and views'. We could add to this 'I have a right to my own thoughts and feelings'. It would be a terrible world if these rights did not exist. There are some regimes around the world where it is not allowed to air your opinions, views, thoughts and feelings but even there no one can stop people having those thoughts, feelings, views and opinions.

We all make sense of the world through our senses – sight, hearing, taste, touch, and smell. We are bombarded with stimuli e.g. words, actions, objects, and events. We use our senses to process the stimuli and our brains give interpretation and meaning to the processed stimuli.

In the chapter on paradigms and heuristics we explored how that interpretation and meaning is affected by our personal biases and expectations.

We also, all experience the world from our own perspective. We have no choice.

You may have seen the cartoon of a group of blindfolded people touching an elephant and being asked to describe the elephant. Each person is touching a different part of the elephant. The person touching only the elephant's tail says, "An elephant is like a snake." The person touching the elephant's trunk says, "An elephant is like a tree." and the person touching the elephant's body says, "An elephant is like a wall." These things are all true and all false depending on your perspective.

It doesn't matter how much someone else does not want us to have our own views, feelings, thoughts and opinions, we cannot help but have them.

An assertive person believes their views, thoughts, feeling and opinions, are just as valid from their own perspective as the thoughts, views, opinions and feelings of anyone else. This does not mean an assertive person believes they are always right. When an assertive person expresses their thoughts, opinions, views or feelings, they are saying, "This is how I feel/think/believe at the moment with the information presented." Assertive people do not believe their views, thoughts, opinions or feelings are more important than those of other people and they are prepared to change their views etc. if new information is presented or if information is presented in a different way.

What Are 'I' Statements?

'I' statements are sentences that often begin with 'I'. Statements that start with phrases such as:

- I believe that...
- I think that...
- I feel that...

In an 'I' statement you are expressing your thoughts, views, opinions and feelings from a personal perspective.

Compare the following statements:

"That is a stupid idea."

And

"I am concerned about that idea."

When you say to another person "That is a stupid idea." What do they hear?

They probably hear you saying to them "You are stupid." You have stated it as fact "That is a stupid idea." It is a judgement on both the idea and the person who came up with the idea. Since you have stated it as a fact you have given the other person little choice except to challenge and say, "No it isn't." Even if the originator now has some doubts about the idea, they cannot allow the personal challenge that they are stupid to go unchallenged.

This is likely to escalate the conflict beyond the original proposed idea.

When you say, "I am concerned about the idea." you are talking about yourself, **not** the other person. You are expressing your feelings about the idea. You are not expressing it as a fact. You are merely pointing out how you feel about the idea from your current perspective. There is room for discussion. Most importantly there is no hint of criticism of the person who originated the idea.

'I' statements do not try to judge, threaten, or control the other person. They do not require you to impose your views on others. They simply report your feelings, thoughts, opinions or beliefs.

It is quite difficult to challenge an 'I' statement.

When you say "That is a stupid idea." it is easy for the other person to say, "No it isn't."

When you say, "I have some concerns about that idea." it is hard for the other person to say, "No you don't." How can another person tell you whether or not you have concerns? It is more likely that when you say, "I have some concerns about that." that the most likely response is "Oh really? What are those concerns?" and you now have permission to voice your concerns.

How To Construct An 'I' Statement

Some people use 'I' statements without realising they are doing so.

For others, when they first start using 'I' statements it may feel a little unnatural.

When constructing an 'I' statement the following process may help.

Step 1

Start your sentence with the word 'I'.

Step 2

Follow the word 'I' with an expression of your thoughts, feelings, beliefs opinions etc.

Here are some examples:

- I feel that...
- I think that...
- I believe that...
- I am afraid that...
- I have some concerns that...
- I have some doubts about...
- I am not sure that...

- I don't agree with that...
- I find that...
- I appreciate that...
- I don't accept that...

Step 3

Then add the action, event or behaviour to your sentence.

i.e.

- I feel that the project has gone off track.
- I think that could work.
- I believe that is not what the contract said.
- I am afraid that we will lose customers by doing this.
- I have some concerns about the proposal.
- I have some doubts about the new process.
- I am not sure that I fully understand the next steps.
- I don't agree with that assessment.
- I find that does not match my experience.
- I appreciate that a lot of effort went into this report.
- I don't accept that is always the case.

Step 4

Follow your 'I' statement' with a request to discuss the situation further.

i.e.

- Can we discuss this please?
- Could we explore this together?
- Could we take some time to talk about it?
- Could we explore some (other) options?
- Could you help me to understand?

Avoid 'You' Statements

When dealing with difficult people be sensitive about the pronouns you use. In particular be aware of 'you' and 'your'.

It is possible to consider 'you' or 'your' as the verbal equivalent of pointing your finger at someone.

- You are wrong...
- You know what your problem is...
- You are being unreasonable...
- You don't understand...
- You are deliberately being difficult...
- You are making me angry...

'You' statements are often perceived as antagonistic, accusatory, threatening and they can give the impression you are trying to control, criticise and judge the other person. This will inevitably provoke a reaction from the other person.

When dealing with difficult people and sensitive situations, it is best to avoid 'you' statements.

Be Careful How You Use 'You' or 'Your' In Your 'I' Statements

It is possible to construct a perfect 'I' statement and have it undermined by including an unnecessary 'you' or 'your' in your sentence.

e.g.

- I have some concerns about your proposal.
- I don't agree with your assessment.
- I don't agree with you.

'Your' is a possessive pronoun. It clearly apportions ownership of the proposal or assessment to the other person.

Even if this is true, it is not always helpful to point it out.

"I don't agree with your assessment." could easily be interpreted as a personal attack.

Just changing it to "I don't agree with that assessment." allows the other person to save face by distancing themselves from the assessment. The subsequent discussion will be on the assessment and not on the person who wrote it.

The same principle applies to

"I don't agree with you."

By using the word 'you', you are implying you disagree with their whole person. You didn't say it, but a particularly sensitive individual might take that to mean you disagree with the way they look, they way they behave, the way they dress etc.

In reality you meant you disagree with the sentence, the proposal, the idea, the suggestion made by the other person. But you didn't say that.

If you had said "I don't agree with that idea." or "I don't agree with that suggestion." you explicitly differentiate between the idea/the proposal/the suggestion and the person.

Being aware of, and reducing your use of, 'your' and 'you' can make a huge difference in reducing conflict when dealing with difficult people.

Beware Of Disguised 'You' Statements

A disguised 'You' statement is one where you start the sentence with 'I' but the sentence is not about the feelings, or thoughts of the person making the statement. It is, instead, a thinly disguised judgement about the other person i.e.

- I feel you are being unreasonable.
- I think you are a jerk.

In the first of those two statements the word 'you' is similar to the previous example of "I don't agree with you."

When you say, "I feel you are being unreasonable." is it your intention to convey that you find everything about the other person to be 'unreasonable'? or is it a particular action, statement or behaviour that you find unreasonable?

If it is the former, then this is definitely a 'you' statement as it does aim to criticise, question, judge, belittle the other. If it is the latter, then it is an unclear statement and would still have been better to say, "I find that idea to be unreasonable."

The second statement, "I think you are a jerk." is a total 'you' statement despite the fact it starts with 'I'.

It is impossible to interpret this as anything other than an attack on the entirety of the other.

Avoid disguised 'You' statements.

How Might You Rewrite The Following As 'I' Statements?

Suggested answers are on the next page.

1. "You have no idea what you are talking about."
2. "Will you just shut up?"
3. "You are the worst neighbour I have ever had."
4. "That is the most stupid idea I have ever heard."
5. "You are making no sense at all."
6. "Your proposal just won't work."
7. "You should not talk to me like that. You are so disrespectful."
8. "You don't care about following the correct process. You just want an easy solution."
9. "You need to be more careful in what you are offering and promising to the customer. You need to agree more realistic deadlines."
10. "You don't really believe your assistant is capable of handling that project, do you?"

Answers:

1. "You have no idea what you are talking about." Rewritten as an 'I' statement could be "I believe the situation is more complex than that. I think we should explore it further."

2. "Will you just shut up." Rewritten as an 'I' statement could be "I don't want to continue this discussion at the moment."

3. "You are the worst neighbour I have ever had." Rewritten as an 'I' statement could be "I am not happy with the situation between us."

4. "That is the most stupid idea I have ever heard." Rewritten as an 'I' statement could be "I am not convinced about that idea."

5. "You are making no sense at all." Rewritten as an 'I' statement could be "I do not understand."

6. "Your proposal will not work." Rewritten as an 'I' statement could be "I do not believe that proposal will work."

7. "You should not talk to me like that. You are so disrespectful." Rewritten as an 'I' statement could be "I do not appreciate being spoken to like that. I find it very disrespectful."

8. "You don't care about following the correct process. You just want an easy solution." Rewritten as an 'I' statement could be "I am convinced it is important

to follow the correct process. I don't believe there are any easy solutions here."

9. "You need to be more careful in what you are offering and promising to the customer. You need to agree to more realistic deadlines." Rewritten as an 'I' statement could be "I think it is important to be careful what we offer to the customer and to make sure any agreed deadlines are realistic."
10. "You don't really believe your assistant is capable of handling that project, do you?" Rewritten as an 'I' statement could be "I have some doubts as to whether your assistant can handle this project. Can we discuss this please?"

Number 8 in that exercise is worth further comment.

“You don’t care about following the process. You just want an easy solution.”

These two sentences are examples of ‘mind reading.’

In both sentences you are telling the other person what is going on in their head.

"You don’t care about..." We have no way of knowing what somebody else cares about.

"You just want..." We have no way of knowing what somebody else really wants unless they tell us.

Any sentence or statement where you are trying to tell somebody what is going on in their own head is doomed to failure. All the other person has to say is, “That’s not true.” and your argument is ruined.

Using "mind-reading" statements like "I know what you're thinking." or "You don't care about anybody but yourself." when dealing with difficult people can be counterproductive for several reasons:

Assumption Of Understanding:

These statements assume you know what the other person is thinking or feeling without confirmation. This can lead to misunderstandings and resentment because you may not accurately perceive their thoughts or emotions.

Invalidation Of Feelings:

Such statements can invalidate the other person's feelings and experiences by dismissing them as known or understood without actually listening to their perspective. This can escalate conflicts and make the other person defensive.

Defensive Reactions:

When people feel their thoughts or feelings are being misrepresented or misunderstood, they often become defensive. This can escalate tensions and hinder effective communication and conflict resolution.

Closed Communication:

Mind-reading statements can shut down communication, rather than opening it up. They may make the other person feel their perspective isn't valued or considered, leading to further breakdowns in communication.

Negative Labeling:

Statements like "You don't care about anybody but yourself." can be perceived as personal attacks or negative labeling, which can damage relationships and trust.

Instead of using mind-reading statements, it's important to focus on open and empathetic communication. This involves active listening and asking clarifying questions to better understand the other person's perspective. Validating their feelings and experiences can help to defuse tension and create a more constructive dialogue.

Chapter 7

Active Listening

Effective listening is one of the most important skills when working to deal with difficult people.

It is said that very few people in the world really listen. The vast majority of us just wait to speak.

This seems to be increasingly true of our global society. Thanks to the rise of social media, everybody now has a voice. But when was the last time you heard anybody say, everybody has an ear?

In fact, we have two ears. Remember the adage, "We have two ears and one mouth. We should use them in the same ratio." In other words we should listen twice as much as we speak.

When did you last watch a political debate on TV where two opponents debated and one of them concluded by saying, “Yes you make some interesting points. You have won me over to your side of the argument?” It often seems as though both parties enjoyed shouting their points but neither side was really prepared to listen to the other.

Why is listening so difficult?

Paradigms And Heuristics...Again

As we have discussed, our paradigms and heuristics make it difficult to listen properly. Our brains process that which we hear through the filter of paradigms and heuristics to select only that information which we like, we agree with, we expected to hear, we have heard before etc.

Preparing Our Response

Our brains work much faster than our mouths. This means that even as someone else is speaking, our brain is deciding what we are going to say when they have finished talking.

The other person may be informing us of an issue e.g. a complaint or a problem and expecting us to provide a solution once they have finished speaking.

We may be afraid of appearing stupid unless we have an appropriately intelligent response. Instead of listening with our full attention, we are busy preparing our solution.

It's also possible, especially in a social situation, that we are not emotionally engaged in what our dialogue partner is saying and are really waiting for them to finish so we can change the subject to something less boring.

Whatever the reason, it won't change the reality that we are trying to do two things at the same time i.e. listening and preparing to speak.

Sadly, most humans cannot do two intellectual things at the same time. It may be possible to walk and talk at the same time or to eat and watch TV, as long as one of the activities can be done mindlessly or on autopilot.

It is possible to walk without concentration or to eat without focusing on the food on your plate, BUT it is practically impossible for the majority of us to give full attention to a speaker whilst intellectually preparing a logically sound argument in response.

What many call 'multi-tasking' is 'task-switching'. We give some of our concentration to one task for a short while, then we switch our focus to the other task for a short while, moving back and forth between the two tasks as we go. In doing so, both tasks suffer.

The consequence of this is that it is virtually impossible for most of us to listen effectively and to prepare our response.

We can do one or the other but not both.

Active listening involves fully engaging with, and comprehending, what someone is saying, both verbally and non-verbally. It goes beyond simply hearing words to truly understanding the message being conveyed. Here's an outline of the skills involved in active listening along with brief descriptions of each:

Attending:

This involves giving full attention to the speaker, making eye contact, facing them directly, and showing genuine interest in what they are saying. Attending demonstrates respect and signals to the speaker that you are fully present.

Withholding Judgement:

Active listening requires setting aside personal biases, prejudices, and preconceptions. It involves suspending judgement about the speaker and their message, allowing them to express themselves freely without fear of criticism.

Reflecting:

Reflecting involves paraphrasing or summarising what the speaker has said to demonstrate understanding and confirm that you have accurately grasped their message. Reflecting can also involve acknowledging the speaker's emotions and validating their feelings.

Empathising:

Empathy involves understanding and sharing the feelings and perspectives of the speaker. It requires putting yourself in their shoes and recognising their emotions without necessarily agreeing with them. Empathising helps establish rapport and engenders trust in the communication process.

Clarifying:

Clarifying involves asking open-ended questions or seeking clarification when something is unclear or ambiguous. It helps ensure mutual understanding and prevents misunderstandings from derailing the conversation.

Summarising:

Summarising involves synthesising key points or themes from the speaker's message to provide a concise overview of what has been discussed. Summarising can help reinforce understanding, identify common ground, and move the conversation forward.

Responding Appropriately:

Responding appropriately involves providing feedback, validation, or support in a manner that is constructive and respectful. It may involve offering encouragement, praise, or reassurance, depending on the context and needs of the speaker.

Maintaining Non-Verbal Cues:

Non-verbal cues such as nodding, maintaining eye contact, and using facial expressions to show interest and understanding are essential components of active listening. Non-verbal cues can enhance communication and convey empathy and engagement.

Resisting Distractions:

Active listening requires focusing solely on the speaker and resisting the urge to be distracted by external stimuli or internal thoughts. It involves maintaining concentration and staying present in the moment to fully engage with the speaker and their message.

Being Patient:

Patience is crucial in active listening, especially when dealing with complex or emotionally charged topics. It involves allowing the speaker to express themselves at their own pace without rushing or interrupting them.

Developing and honing these skills can greatly enhance one's ability to engage in active listening and facilitate effective communication in various personal and professional contexts.

Chapter 8

Effective Questioning

Good quality questioning is a vital skill in your toolkit for dealing with difficult people.

There are two main reasons for this:

Gaining More Information:

If you are going to deal with a difficult situation it is likely that one, or a combination of any, of the following has happened:

- The other person is unhappy.
- They have a problem they want solved.
- They have a complaint.
- There is something about what you have done or said that they find objectionable.
- Something has happened that is not in line with

their expectations.

Irrespective of which situation (or combination of situations) have caused the difficult situation, the first approach is to gather more information.

Questions are the best way to discover this information.

You will need to establish:

- Why are they unhappy?
- What is the problem that needs solving?
- What is the nature of the complaint?
- What did you do or say that they found objectionable?
- What happened and how did it differ from their expectations?

De-escalating The Emotions:

It can be very difficult to deal with difficult people in a highly charged emotional situation. For many, it can be a nightmare to deal with someone who is shouting, being angry, or demonstrating verbally abusive or threatening behaviour.

One way of de-escalating the emotions is to move the other person into a problem-solving mode. The first response of a human being to almost any situation is an emotional response. It takes time and energy for us to move beyond the emotional and into the logical, rational centres of the brain. The problem-solving centres are generally less emotional. If we can engage the other person in a problem-solving activity it is likely the emotions will de-escalate.

When we ask a question, we require the other person to find an appropriate answer. If your question is a good quality open-ended question, then it will almost always cause the person to engage the problem-solving centres of their brain to search for the answer. This begins the process of emotional de-escalation.

Types Of Questions:

There are many different types of questions but here we will deal with the three main types. If you can master each of these three types you will be well-served in your difficult conversations.

Closed-ended Questions:

Closed-ended questions are questions that typically require a specific, brief answer, often a simple "yes" or "no" or a short factual response. These questions are designed to elicit specific information and do not encourage elaboration or discussion. Closed-ended questions are commonly used in surveys, interviews, and situations where precise information is needed quickly.

Examples of closed-ended questions:

Yes/No Questions:

- "Did you enjoy the movie?"
- "Have you ever been to Paris?"
- "Is it raining outside?"

Multiple Choice Questions:

- "Which colour do you prefer: red, blue, or green?"
- "Which of the following is not a mammal: fish, cat, dog, or horse?"
- "What time works best for our meeting: 9 a.m., 11 a.m., or 2 p.m.?"

Likert Scale Questions (A type of closed-ended question that asks respondents to indicate their level of agreement or disagreement on a scale):

- "On a scale of 1 to 5, how satisfied are you with our customer service?"
- "How likely are you to recommend our product to a friend or colleague: very likely, somewhat likely, neither likely nor unlikely, somewhat unlikely, or very unlikely?"

Numeric Response Questions:

- "How many siblings do you have?"
- "What is the temperature outside right now?"

Closed-ended questions are effective for gathering specific information quickly and efficiently. However, they may limit the depth of response and may not capture nuances or complexities in the respondent's viewpoint.

Despite most people knowing about, and understanding the concept of open-ended questions, it is still common for people to ask too many closed-ended questions. One of the reasons for this may be that people think they are asking an open-ended question when they are, in fact, asking a closed-ended question.

“Is there anything else I should know?” feels like an open-ended question but it isn’t.

Closed-ended questions are not bad. They have their uses. But the problem with asking too many closed-ended questions in a difficult conversation is that it puts most of the work on the questioner. The questioner is constantly trying to think of the next question to ask. This makes it difficult to listen to the answers. It can also make a difficult person more difficult in that they feel they are being interrogated.

Open-Ended Questions:

Open-ended questions are questions that prompt a more detailed and expansive response, encouraging the other person to provide their thoughts, opinions, or experiences. Unlike closed-ended questions, which typically elicit short, specific answers, open-ended questions invite individuals to express themselves freely and in their own words. These questions are valuable for encouraging dialogue, exploring complex topics, and gaining deeper insights into the respondent's perspectives.

Open-ended questions typically start with the following words:

- Who?
- What?
- Where?
- When?
- Why?
- How?

They are sometimes referred to as 5WH.

Examples of open-ended questions:

Opinion/Thought-Provoking Questions:

- "What are your thoughts on the current state of the economy?"

- "How do you feel about the new company policy?"
- "What is your opinion on the role of technology in education?"

Exploratory Questions:

- "Can you tell me more about your experience working on that project?"
- "How did you come up with the idea for your novel?"
- "What factors influenced your decision to pursue a career in engineering?"

Reflective Questions:

- "What did you learn from that challenging situation?"
- "How do you think you could improve your communication skills?"
- "In what ways has travel influenced your perspective on different cultures?"

Scenario-Based Questions:

- "What would you do differently if you were in charge of planning this event?"
- "How do you envision the future of renewable energy?"
- "If you could change one thing about your

community, what would it be?"

Feeling/Emotion Questions:

- "How did you feel when you received that award?"
- "What emotions arise for you when you think about your childhood?"
- "What impact did that experience have on your sense of self?"

Open-ended questions encourage deeper exploration, foster meaningful conversation, and allow individuals to express themselves more fully. They are particularly useful in qualitative research, therapeutic settings, and situations where understanding the nuances of someone's perspective is important.

The Exception:

There is an exception to the 5WH approach and that is one of the following:

- Can you tell me...?
- Please tell me...?
- Tell me....

Technically none of these are open-ended questions but they are almost universally accepted as so.

“Can you tell me...?” is technically a closed-ended question.

“Please tell me...” is a request.

“Tell me...” is a command.

But all three can be used to elicit information in the same way as an open-ended question and therefore they might be regarded as 'honorary' open-ended questions.

The Rule Of Open-Ended Questions

The simple rule of asking an open-ended question is...

Ask your question and then...SHUT UP!

Many people start to ask a good quality open-ended question. This is good, Unfortunately they are often so afraid of the silence that follows their question that they commit the ultimate sin in questioning. That sin is to ask a good quality open-ended question and then, without giving the other person a chance to answer, to follow the open-ended question with a closed-ended question.

e.g.

“What is your concern about this? Is it the price?”

“How will you make your decision? Will you discuss it with your wife?”

The open-ended questions were perfect here.

Had the questioner asked the question and then allowed some time for the other person to answer, they would have learned some valuable information.

Imagine you had asked “What is your concern about this?”

Whatever the person had said next would have provided valuable information. They might have revealed a list of concerns. They might have revealed only their major concern. They might not have understood the question and asked you to clarify your question further, but that would also have told you something about their level of understanding.

By following the open-ended question with a closed-ended question you learn much less.

If you had asked "What is your concern about this? Is it the price?" You allowed the other person the opportunity to reply "yes" to the closed-ended part of the question.

It is now difficult to know whether they said "yes" because price is their main concern, or if they said "yes" because *you* introduced the concept of 'price' and they wanted to see how you would react if they said that was their major concern.

They may have said "yes" because they couldn't think of another concern, and you made it easy for them to just say "yes"

You will never be sure exactly what their "yes" means without asking further questions.

As a general rule of thumb, it is a good idea to ask an open-ended question and then to shut up. Wait. Don't interrupt. Don't add a closed-ended question. Don't answer the question yourself.

Just wait.

Probing Questions:

When we speak, we often talk at a surface level. We might say the first thing that comes into our mind, or we might give a flippant answer, or a short non-committal answer.

In a difficult situation it is possible that the other person wants to hold their cards close to their chest and not give away unnecessary information. They may be reluctant to co-operate with your first question.

When you ask your open-ended question, you might get an answer but do not then assume you have all the information you need.

You might have asked them, "Why are you unhappy?" and the reply might have been "I am disappointed with the level of service I have received."

It may be tempting to start apologising about the level of service offered but you don't really know what that sentence "I was disappointed by the level of service I received" really means.

Could it mean that the service fell short of expectations? If so, in what way?

Could it mean that the level of service exceeded expectations, and more was delivered than needed? This sounds unlikely but it is not impossible.

Does 'disappointed' mean angry? Or just let down?

Are they disappointed to the point where they don't want to do business with you again? Or is it a mild disappointment that might easily be corrected?

Probing questions are questions designed to delve deeper into a topic, uncover additional information, or clarify points raised by the other person. These questions are used to explore details, motivations, or underlying reasons behind a statement or response. Probing questions are particularly useful for gathering comprehensive insights, understanding complex issues, and facilitating meaningful dialogue.

Examples Of Probing Questions:

- "Can you provide more details about that aspect?"
- "Why do you think this approach is the most effective?"
- "What led you to make that decision?"
- "How do you feel about the situation, and why?"
- "Could you elaborate on how this issue has affected your team dynamics?"
- "What obstacles do you anticipate encountering as you work toward your goal?"
- "Can you give an example to illustrate your point?"
- "What factors influenced your opinion on this matter?"
- "How do you think this solution aligns with our

long-term objectives?"

- "What alternatives did you consider before arriving at this conclusion?"

Probing questions encourage individuals to reflect, expand on their responses, and provide deeper insights into their thoughts, feelings, and experiences. They are commonly used in interviews, coaching sessions, problem-solving discussions, and research enquiries to uncover valuable information and facilitate a more thorough understanding of a topic or situation.

Your probing questions will be guided by the answers the other has given in response to your open-ended questions.

As you listen to their answer, listen for the following:

- What's missing?
- What is unclear?
- What is open to interpretation?

Don't assume you know exactly what they mean without asking.

Chapter 9

Strategies For Dealing With Different Types Of Difficult People

Navigating interactions with difficult people can often feel like traversing a minefield, each step fraught with the potential for conflict or misunderstanding. In the realm of human interaction, personalities vary widely, and encountering individuals who present challenges is inevitable. However, how we choose to respond to these challenges can greatly influence the outcome of our interactions and the quality of our relationships.

In this section of the book, we delve into the intricacies of dealing with different types of difficult people, offering a nuanced exploration of strategies tailored to specific personality archetypes. From the confrontational tactics of Bullies and Dominators to the frustrating encounters with

Always-Right Autocrats, this is a toolkit for navigating the myriad of personalities we may encounter in our personal and professional lives.

It's essential to approach these strategies with a discerning eye, recognising that no single approach fits all situations. Every interaction is unique, shaped by individual dynamics, contextual factors, and personal boundaries. Therefore, the strategies presented here are not prescriptions but rather options for consideration, offering food for thought as you navigate the complexities of human relationships.

As you delve into the following sections, remember that the choice of response ultimately rests with you. Each strategy outlined is but a thread in the rich tapestry of interpersonal communication, to be woven into the fabric of your own approach according to your judgement and the specific nuances of the situation at hand. By approaching difficult interactions with mindfulness and adaptability, we empower ourselves to increase understanding, resolve conflicts, and cultivate healthier relationships.

Chapter 10

Bullies And Dominators

It is unlikely any of us will go through our entire lives without encountering someone we regard as a bully or someone who wants to dominate us.

We may have encountered our first bully at school. When we left school, we rather hoped we had also left the bullies behind.

Sadly, that often proves not to be the case.

Your difficult person may be a domineering boss or colleague. It could be your worst client, an awkward neighbour, a family member or even your own partner.

These people can make us totally miserable.

There is no single way to deal with every one of these.

You will probably react to a domineering boss or client differently than you would to a neighbour or a family member.

There is an old expression that says "If the only tool in your toolkit is a hammer, then every problem looks like a nail."

If you have only one way of reacting to a given situation then that is the choice you will make for every event.

When situations go wrong it is normally because we have chosen the wrong approach.

Broadening our strategic choices improves our chances of finding the correct approach.

Nobody gets it right all the time and there is no one approach that works with everybody. This is a good thing. Imagine if this book did contain a technique that would allow you win in every situation. The chances are your difficult people would have bought this book and would be using those techniques to dominate you even more.

The following strategies are there for you to have more tools in your toolkit.

Which of them you choose will depend on the relationship and the situation.

But before you do anything you must control your own emotions.

When we encounter a bully our 'fight or flight' mechanism triggers as effectively as it would if we were facing a lion, a tiger or a bear.

The 'fight' response might cause us to get angry and lash out at the bully. We might:

- Say things we shouldn't say
- Say things we didn't mean
- Swear
- Use insulting or unprofessional language

We might use threatening physical behaviour such as:

- Finger pointing
- Pushing
- Invading personal space
- In extremes, a punch might be thrown

All these are likely to escalate the situation for all parties and the outcome is unlikely to be satisfactory. Inevitably they will take you all past the point of no return.

Whilst this may sometimes be the only option, the outcome is unpredictable. It could cause you to get fired from your job, cause you to lose a client or even lose your partner.

The 'flight' part of the response might cause you to:

- Freeze
- Find it hard to talk
- Leave the room

- Just accept the bullying behaviour
- Get upset
- Get depressed

All these responses are unhelpful when it comes to addressing bullying.

The first thing we need to do, therefore, is to get our emotional responses under control.

This is harder than it seems.

In his amazing book, Thinking, Fact and Slow, Daniel Kahneman[1] describes the 2 systems that operate in response to external stimuli.

System 1 is often the first system to operate. This system operates very quickly and requires very little energy.

System 1 is the emotional response. It is the system responsible for the 'fight or flight' mechanism.

The other system, System 2, is the system responsible for the logical, rational, problem solving and decision-making behaviours.

Unfortunately this system is slower and takes more energy to operate.

Kahneman is not the only person to describe this process.

---

1. Thinking, Fast And Slow by Daniel Kahneman, Penguin Publishers

It is also referenced in 'TheTriune Brain'[2]

This describes the development of the brain in three different areas.

The Reptilian Brain

The earliest part of the brain to be developed was the reptilian complex. The "reptilian brain" refers to the most primitive part of the brain, which is primarily composed of the brainstem and the basal ganglia. This term is derived from the idea that this part of the brain is evolutionarily similar to the brains of reptiles. It is responsible for regulating basic survival functions and instinctual behaviours. The reptilian brain is sometimes referred to as the "old brain" or the "primitive brain."

Some examples of functions associated with the reptilian brain include:

Survival Instincts:

The reptilian brain is responsible for the instinctual responses necessary for survival, such as the fight-or-flight response. When faced with a threat, this part of the brain triggers physiological changes designed to prepare the body to either confront the threat or flee from it.

---

2. The **Triune Brain** is a model developed by the American physician Paul. D. MacLean

Basic Bodily Functions:

The reptilian brain regulates essential bodily functions such as breathing, heart rate, and blood pressure. These functions are critical for maintaining life and are largely automated processes that do not require conscious thought.

Territoriality And Aggression:

This part of the brain is involved in behaviours related to territoriality, dominance, and aggression. It helps regulate behaviours associated with defending territory or asserting dominance within social hierarchies.

Reproduction And Sexual Behaviour:

The reptilian brain also plays a role in regulating reproductive behaviours and sexual impulses. It is involved in the instinctual drive to seek out mates and engage in mating behaviours.

Basic Emotions:

The reptilian brain is associated with basic emotions such as fear, anger, and pleasure. These emotions are essential for survival and are closely linked to the instinctual responses triggered by the fight-or-flight system.

Habit Formation And Routine Behaviours:

The reptilian brain is involved in the formation of habits and routine behaviours. It helps automate repetitive actions, allowing individuals to conserve cognitive resources for more complex tasks.

Overall, the reptilian brain serves as the foundation for many of our most basic survival instincts and behaviours.

The Limbic Brain

The next part of the brain to develop was the limbic brain. It emerged in the first mammals. The limbic brain, also known as the limbic system, is a complex set of brain structures located beneath the cerebral cortex. It plays a crucial role in regulating emotions, memory, and certain aspects of behaviour. Often referred to as the "emotional brain," the limbic system is involved in processing and interpreting emotional stimuli and generating emotional responses.

Some examples of functions associated with the limbic brain include:

Emotional Processing:

The limbic system is responsible for processing and regulating emotions. It helps to interpret emotional cues from the environment and generates appropriate emotional responses. Structures within the limbic system, such as the amygdala and the hippocampus, play key roles in emotional processing.

Memory Formation And Retrieval:

The limbic system is involved in the formation and retrieval of memories, particularly those with emotional significance. The hippocampus, in particular, is critical for the formation of new memories, while the amygdala helps to encode emotionally charged memories and retrieve them when similar emotional stimuli are encountered.

Reward And Motivation:

The limbic system plays a central role in the brain's reward system, which regulates motivation and pleasure.

Stress Response:

The limbic system is involved in the body's response to stress and threat. The amygdala, in particular, plays a key role in initiating the body's stress response by triggering the release of stress hormones such as cortisol and adrenaline.

Regulation Of Autonomic Functions:

While the brain stem primarily regulates autonomic functions such as heart rate, respiration, and digestion, the limbic system can also influence these functions, particularly in response to emotional stimuli. For example, experiencing fear or anxiety can lead to changes in heart rate and respiration mediated by the limbic system.

Social And Attachment Behaviours:

The limbic system is involved in regulating social behaviours, attachment, and bonding.

Overall, the limbic system plays a vital role in regulating many aspects of human behaviour and cognition, particularly those related to emotions, memory, and motivation.

The limbic system and the prehistoric stem combine to form the 'primitive' brain.

The Neocortex

This is the newest part of the brain. It accounts for 85% of the human brain's total mass. It is what makes us human. The neocortex, also known as the cerebral cortex, is the outermost layer of the brain and is the most recent part of the brain in evolutionary terms. It is highly developed in humans and is responsible for many higher-order brain functions, including sensory perception, motor control, cognition, and language.

Some examples of functions associated with the neocortex include:

Sensory Perception:

The neocortex receives and processes sensory information from the environment, including sight, sound, touch, taste, and smell.

Motor Control:

The neocortex is involved in planning, initiating, and coordinating voluntary movements. Motor commands generated in the neocortex are sent to the appropriate muscles via the motor pathways, enabling precise and coordinated movements.

Cognition And Higher Order Thinking:

The neocortex plays a crucial role in cognitive functions such as attention, perception, memory, reasoning, and problem-solving. It allows us to analyse information, make decisions, and adapt to changing circumstances.

Language Processing:

Specific regions of the neocortex, particularly in the left hemisphere, are specialised for language processing. These regions are involved in understanding and producing spoken and written language, as well as in other aspects of language, such as grammar and syntax.

Executive Functions:

The neocortex is involved in executive functions, which include abilities such as planning, organising, goal-setting, inhibiting impulses, and self-regulation. These functions are critical for goal-directed behaviour and self-control.

Emotional Regulation:

While the limbic system primarily regulates emotions, the neocortex also plays a role in emotional regulation. Regions of the prefrontal cortex, in particular, are involved in modulating emotional responses and regulating emotional expression.

Social Cognition:

The neocortex is involved in processing social information and understanding the thoughts, feelings, and intentions of others.

Overall, the neocortex is responsible for many of the complex cognitive abilities that distinguish humans from other animals. It's highly developed structure and diverse functions allow us to perceive, understand, and interact with the world in sophisticated ways.

The Differences Between The Primitive Brain And The Neocortex

The primitive brain requires little energy to operate quickly. The higher brain is more powerful but requires a lot of energy to run and operates more slowly than the primitive brain. This is because the primitive brain is primarily responsible for regulating basic survival functions and instinctual responses, which require rapid processing to ensure immediate reactions to threats or opportunities for survival.

On the other hand, the neocortex, being the outer layer of the brain responsible for higher-order cognitive functions, operates at a slower speed and consumes more energy. This is because the neocortex is involved in complex processes such as decision-making, problem-solving, and language processing, which require more neural connections and energy to carry out.

In the real world, this difference in speed and energy consumption between the primitive brain and the neocortex may explain why our emotional responses and related physical responses tend to kick in before reason and logic can take control.

Have you ever been in an argument with a friend, your boss or a colleague and said things you later wish you had not said. Perhaps you may have been so upset or embarrassed that you didn't say anything. In either case it was likely to be your primitive brain operating. It's that feeling when the 'red mist' descends when you are angry, or you blush or your voice starts to quiver or you feel your eyes watering.

Later, when you have calmed down you start to think "I wish I had said this..." or "I wish I had answered that..."

This is when your neocortex has had time to catch up and is now operating.

The challenge when dealing with difficult people is to get your emotions under control so that your neocortex can start to help you in handling the particular situation in which you find yourself.

Getting Your Emotions Under Control

When dealing with bullies we need to start by keeping control of our emotions.

The work of Kahneman, MacLean and others demonstrate the emotional centres of our brain will operate long before logic and reason can kick in. It is clear, therefore, that when faced with bullying behaviour from others, we need to allow some time for the neocortex to catch up and take control.

Breathe

When you were a child and you felt yourself getting angry or losing your temper it is possible the adults around you may have said something like "Take a breath and count to 10." This is, on reflection, very sound advice.

Try a simple exercise.

Take a deep breath.

Then tense up your entire body. Make sure every part of you is as tense as you can be.

Now breathe out and try to remain tense.

Not easy is it?

It is highly likely that, as you breathed out, your body began to relax. You can just about keep it tense with concentration, but it is not easy.

When you were told to "Breathe and count to 10." the breathing would have helped to have reduced some of the tension in your body.

Counting to 10 takes time. This short time may be enough to allow the neocortex to catch up with the emotional 'primitive' brain.

Take A Break

Taking a breath and counting to 10 doesn't give you much time to get your emotions in check. You may need more time.

For this you may need to create a break of some kind.

If you are in a difficult meeting with your boss, customer, supplier, or colleague you might say something like "I need to check some details. Let me go and get the documents I need. I will be back in a couple of minutes." That couple of minutes may give you the time you need to compose yourself.

If it is outside of work, you might want to excuse yourself to visit the washroom to give you the time you need.

Bullies will not want to give you the time to compose, so you must insist. It often suits their purpose to have you flustered or emotionally disturbed. You need to be firm on obtaining a break.

If you need the washroom, you need the washroom. If the other party is demanding answers from you, then you need to consult those documents outside the room.

The bully may appear angry or annoyed by this but remember that is part of their bullying behaviour.

Once you have got your emotions in check there are variety of options open to you for dealing with the bullying behaviour:

Bring It Into The Open

It seems incredible to the victims of bullying that sometimes bullies do not know they are bullies.

It is not always a conscious act.

People with control issues can sometimes end up acting in a bullying manner as a consequence of their desire to control the situation.

They do not mean to hurt anyone, but some people are so afraid of losing control that they panic if the situation gets out of their control. That panic can cause them to over-react and speak badly to those around them. They don't mean to be domineering, they just want the situation back under control. It can be purely a reaction to stress.

Others believe they are being 'extremely assertive'. They will often use phrases like "I am a straight-talking person." or "I believe in being direct." or "Let's not waste time".

They don't see themselves as bullies at all. They dislike people who are hesitant or lacking in confidence. They may be completely unaware of their domineering and bullying attitude.

The best technique for dealing with people like this is to bring it into the open and discuss it with them.

Be assertive and use your 'I' statements.

e.g.

"I'd like to have a word about the way you spoke to me in the meeting last week. When you told everyone the report looked as though it had been written by a three year old I felt humiliated and embarrassed. I would like to discuss with you about why that happened."

It is important you clearly explain your feelings about the behaviour and its impact on you.

Focus completely on what was said or done. It is equally important that you do not fight fire with fire and try to counter-attack the bully.

Do not add judgements to the behaviour.

e.g. it is acceptable to say, "In our weekly meeting you described my department as incompetent."

You are on less solid ground if you say, "You disrespected my leadership by describing my department as incompetent."

This is just likely to escalate a volatile situation.

You could say "I felt disrespected."

In confronting the other person, you may alert them to the effects of their behaviour.

Nobody really likes to think of themselves as bad people. In alerting them you may have brought their attention to the unforeseen consequences of trying to maintain control.

This may be all it takes to change your bully to a reasonable and positive presence in your life.

Positive Reinforcement

In 2004 a reality-based TV series made its debut on Channel 4 in the UK. It was called Supernanny.

In the TV series, author and nanny, Jo Frost helped parents deal with problematic parenting issues.

Despite the series running for 8 seasons, the advice given was remarkably consistent. One of the central themes for good parenting was:

Don't reward the behaviour you don't want. Reward the behaviour you do want

Imagine a child asks for an ice cream and you say, "No." The child then throws themselves on the floor and begins to scream and cry for an ice cream. If, in embarrassment, and to shut up the child, the parents say "OK, OK, I will let you have an ice cream." the child has just been educated that if they want an ice cream they only need to throw a tantrum until the parent gives in.

This is unwise. When that child grows up, this learned behaviour may transform into bullying others i.e. scream at them until they give you what you want.

This bully learned early in life that, if they want something, they need to throw the equivalent of an adult tantrum until the other person concedes the point.

This behaviour needs to be changed. Sadly, if the bullying behaviour is directed towards you, it is in your interests to do what the child's parents did not. You must not reward bad behaviour.

How does this work in practice?

We all have many choices as to how we respond to requests.

Sometimes we can refuse to comply completely. This is often possible when receiving requests or commands from family, friends, or neighbours.

If the request is made in a way that is unacceptable to you, you could say, "No." and refuse to do it at all until asked in a way that is more acceptable to you.

This is something parents often teach their children at a young age.

e.g.

Child: "I want a drink of water."

Parent: "What's the magic word?"

Child: "Please."

You might take this approach with your bully. If asked in a bullying or patronising or insulting manner you might refuse to comply until the language, tone or approach is changed.

For some, this is too confrontational, even with family members. It would be very difficult to use this with your boss or your clients or even your colleagues.

In a professional environment we are often required, through our contracts of employment, to respond to requests from managers, colleagues, and clients. Our contracts don't always specify the manner in which the request must be made.

More and more organisations are introducing 'codes of conduct' into the workplace. These specify treating each other with courtesy and respect. Since most contracts do require employees to adhere to these codes of conduct, we could argue treating each other with respect is now part of the contract, but it is a subjective judgement. It can be hard to prove that when your boss says, "Would you mind doing that please?" in a sarcastic tone of voice, they are being disrespectful. You know they are. They know they are, but on paper the words look fine.

This leaves us with a dilemma.

Our contract demands we respond to requests.

But there are many ways we can respond, even within our contractual constraints.

We could respond by:

- Being enthusiastic
- Being eager
- Beating the deadline
- Delivering more than requested
- Providing helpful but unsolicited suggestions and advice

OR, we could stay within the realms of our contract and still respond by:

- Only providing what is asked
- Offering no extra information
- Delivering on the deadline (even if earlier was possible)
- Adhering strictly to the rules of the contract or agreement
- Behaving in a neutral manner (not unpleasant but not enthusiastic or eager either)

Why does this matter?

Human beings need response.

Almost all human behaviour is focused towards getting a response from others.

When we smile at a person, we hope the person will smile back.

When we talk to someone else, we want to feel they are listening and value what we say. We expect to see them nod in agreement, make noises of encouragement. We want them to maintain eye contact and to face us when we are talking to them. We hope they might laugh or smile.

If we speak and we receive little or no encouragement, we feel like we are wasting our time. It can be devastating to receive no response from others.

I used to do an exercise on my training courses that I had to stop since it became too emotional.

This was the exercise.

I divided participants into 2 groups.

Group A:

Participants in this group were to think of their favourite book, holiday, or movie. They had to pair up with one of the people in Group B and to try to persuade them to watch this movie, buy this book or go on this holiday.

To the participants in Group A this appeared to be an exercise about their ability to persuade or sell.

Group B had different instructions.

Group B:

Participants in this group were asked to pair up with someone else from Group A and listen to what they had to say (I did not tell them what Group A were going to say)

BUT when their partner from Group A was talking, the task of Group B participants was to ignore them. Not to maintain eye contact, not to respond, smile, nod, ask questions or respond in any way.

I thought the purpose of the exercise would become obvious to the participants in Group A quickly and they would appreciate how difficult it was to speak to someone who did not respond.

I was surprised, however, at the strength of feeling it raised.

When I took feedback after the exercise, participants from Group B normally found the exercise funny and had enjoyed ignoring their partner. For them it wasn't too serious an exercise.

For participants from Group A, however, they were often deeply unsettled by the experience. They understood the intellectual point of the exercise, but many took some time to calm down from the frustration and anger they had felt at being ignored.

Human beings need response.

I once heard of a group of students who decided to practise the effects of response on their lecturer.

The lecturer did not know what the students were doing.

When the lecture began, the students observed where the lecturer was standing.

If the lecturer stood on the left side of the room the students looked up, they smiled, they nodded, they made notes, they asked questions, they engaged fully in the lecture.

If, however, the lecturer stood on the right side of the room, the students put down their pens, stopped smiling, stopped asking questions and stopped engaging in the lecture.

They noted that after a short time the lecturer began to present only from the left side of the room.

When one of the students asked, "Professor can I ask why you are presenting from that side of the room?" The lecturer replied that "The light is better on this side of the room."

It is possible the lecturer had subconsciously registered the lack of response and adapted his behaviour accordingly.

This need for response can be very powerful.

And it can be very useful as a way of addressing bullying behaviour.

Whilst you are contractually required to respond to requests from your boss, your colleague, your clients etc, you are NOT contractually required to do more than requested. That is still within your control.

It can be tempting to give our best efforts to our angriest clients and our most demanding bosses. In responding like this, you are behaving like the parent responding to the child having a tantrum over an ice cream. You are educating your boss, your clients and possibly friends, relatives, and neighbours that, to get the most from you, they need to behave badly.

You need to reverse this.

When people behave in a bullying or domineering way towards you, they should receive your minimal response. Only the people who treat you with respect and courtesy will get your maximum response.

A friend once told me of how he used this with a client.

The client was a monster to everyone. The client frequently called to complain that the company was charging him for services he had received. He criticised the company for being expensive (despite the fact the company was well within the market price) and regularly demanded price reductions. In the past he had often received these price reductions because of his bullying behaviour. Sadly, work with this client, had now reached a point where there was no margin for further price reductions. He was no longer an attractive client for the company, and everybody tried to avoid him. The moment the people in the office heard this client was on the phone everyone ran for cover. Suddenly everybody was busy.

Anyone unfortunate enough to fail to find something else to do, ended up with the client yelling and criticising them. Which reinforced the need to avoid the client on the next occasion.

This was a lose/lose for both parties.

The company was making no money from this client and didn't want to serve him. The client was getting a low price, but he was getting a minimal service in return.

My friend decided to try 'positive reinforcement'.

In the next conversation with the angry client, my friend made a conscious decision to minimise his responses to the bullying behaviour and to maximise the responses to more friendly and productive behaviour.

The next time the angry client called my friend volunteered to take the call.

As the client screamed and shouted about his latest complaint my friend listened politely and made the required number of conciliatory noises e.g. "I'm sorry to hear that." "I understand how frustrating that must be." but added nothing more than was required. When the client complained about the price my friend remained silent and made no moves to discuss the price or offer any reductions. This was easy since there were no more possible reductions. After some time of shouting the client did eventually run out of steam and said to my friend, "I am sorry for being so angry, but I am sure you appreciate how this feels from my perspective."

It was the most positive thing the client had said, and my friend responded positively by saying, "I do understand, and I am here to help as much as I can." The client responded by saying, "I appreciate that; I don't always feel that from every member of your team." The client then went back to complaining.

The next time the client called, he specifically asked to speak to my friend. Once again, my friend took the call. Once again, the call began with the screaming and shouting, but once the client had 'vented' he actually asked my friend, "And how are you today?" This was something he had never done before.

Over the next few calls, the abuse gradually reduced, and the positive behaviour increased to the point where most of it was collaborative and cooperative. My friend was now proactively making calls to the client offering help and advice. The client was actively seeking to do additional business with the company at a commercially attractive rate and the relationship became more productive for both.

If you are encountering bullying or coercive behaviour from others, you must minimise your response. Do only what is required and no more. If the other person does behave more respectfully towards you, then reward that change in behaviour. Increase your responses and offer more than expected. Show the other person that the best way to get more from you is to treat you well. It may take some time but, in my experience, it often works well.

Escalate and Expose

This response only really works for corporate bullying.

You may try to confront the bully. You may try positive reinforcement. Nothing works every time and with every person.

Some people appear to be born bullies and get a kick from it.

If you have tried all reasonable approaches, you may need to escalate this to your manager or, if your manager is the bully, to HR.

Most organisations take bullying seriously and do not like a bullying culture in the company. I am often asked to provide coaching for the 'bullies' to change their behaviour after a complaint has been made about them.

Do not make this your first approach. It can backfire. It creates an unpleasant environment. The consequences can be severe for everyone involved. You may not like your manager, but do you really want to be responsible for them getting fired? Even if they are fired, you will still have to work with their friends and supporters afterwards. You will also need to be sure you have a case, and you are beyond reproach yourself. Is your manager behaving harshly towards you because you are not doing your job properly?

Take this approach if you can see no more productive alternative.

End The Relationship

The problem with being in a bullying relationship with a partner, family member, neighbour, colleague, boss etc. is that it can infect your whole life.

It's as if there is no alternative and that you must endure it until it ends somehow.

But it can begin to affect your judgement, your moods, and your relationships with others. People who are bullied at work go home and find they cannot enjoy being with their family because they live under the cloud of knowing they must return to work the next day. If you are enduring a bullying relationship at home, it may be impossible to do your best at work and that creates further problems.

As a last resort, if you have tried everything else, you should ask yourself, "Why are you putting up with this?"

It may be difficult to find another job if you leave, but is it better to stay in a bullying relationship at work and making your family unhappy when you get home? Maybe they would be happier with less money coming in but a happier parent. And who knows, once you start looking for another job you might surprise yourself and find a much better job with a much better working environment.

If it's a neighbour, have you considered moving?

A relative of mine lived in a beautiful house in a small village. Unfortunately, there was a disagreement between my relative and a particularly vocal bully. The bully managed to convince their social circle that my relative was at fault. Each day she had to endure comments and jeering remarks at the school gates as she waited to pick up her children each day.

Her children were not invited to parties or outings and she and her husband were aware they were often the topic of less than flattering conversations from their former social circle.

My relative became depressed and lost a lot of confidence. No matter how much she tried to explain her side of the story, the bully managed to override her.

Eventually she and her husband sold the house they loved and moved out of the village. Fortunately, they found a nicer house, in a nicer village, with truly lovely neighbours and I have never seen my relative so happy.

When I have spoken to her since she moved, she often says, "I am glad we moved. I don't know why I put up with that nonsense for so long."

That phrase rings a bell with me.

It is one I have heard so many times from people who have left bad job situations or bullying relationships. When they finally escape, they often say, "I don't know why I put up with that for so long."

The world is a big place. There are lots of places to live. Lots of jobs, and lots of potentially healthier relationships, but you won't find them whilst you are under the thumb of your bully.

So, ending the relationship is another option.

Your final option is:

Let It Go

In every relationship there is a cost/benefit equation.

In a business relationship the equation is balancing the salary or fee you get against the effort and energy you put into the relationship.

In a personal relationship it might be weighing up the level of happiness, fulfilment, joy, love etc you gain against the energy, effort, love, commitment you give.

In a bullying business relationship it is possible that you may decide to endure the bullying behaviour because it is outweighed by the gains you receive.

You may decide to endure a bullying client because they pay extremely well and help you to achieve your targets.

You may decide to endure a bullying boss because the salary is above market expectations and there is potential to advance your career. Many young lawyers in the US make this decision when they join prestigious law firms as first year associates. In their first year they may be worked to the point of exhaustion. It is a ruthless, tough environment with little tolerance for weakness. Only the tough will survive. Many young people will tolerate this bullying behaviour in the hope that one day they will make partner and achieve a life that provides the rewards they seek.

In our personal relationships this can be a harder equation.

With clients and companies, we can see an end to the bullying. Endurance is a means to an end. In personal relationships it can be hard to see this end point.

A person with low self esteem might decide that a bullying partner is better than no partner at all.

A child with bullying parents might decide that bullying love is better than no love at all.

I do not believe this is a healthy decision. One of the other strategies may be better to employ.

It is possible some parents will allow their children to dominate in some situations as a way of helping and encouraging that child to become more independent. This is fine as long as it does not go too far.

Others may understand that bullying behaviour by a partner or a relative masks an underlying cause. For example, a partner or loved one suffering a serious illness and in a lot of pain. They may lash out and be rude and insulting from time to time. Their loved one recognises this is not intentional and is only a symptom of the pain. In this case there might be a decision to 'let it go' but even here it must not be allowed to go too far or for too long.

Some carers can suffer years of abuse at the hands of those for whom they provide care. This might be described as emotional blackmail. The sick person is using their carer's love and care against them. It is not fair and it is not right.

Carers also have a right be treated with love and respect.

So The Right Answer Is...

It depends.

No one strategy will work with every bully and every form of bullying behaviour. Each situation will need to be judged in the context of the relationship and the circumstances. Most situations, however, can be addressed using one or more of the approaches described in this chapter.

Chapter 11

Always-Right Autocrats

This group of people believe there are two views of the world – theirs and 'the wrong one'. You either agree with them or you are just plain wrong. It's as simple as that.

It may stem from an insecurity that the identity of the Always-Right Autocrat is dependent upon the certainty of being correct in every circumstance. It may be an example of controlling behaviour. Maybe they were punished or experienced humiliation as children if they got the answer wrong at school.

It may also stem from a 'fixed-mindset'.

Carol Dweck's book 'Mindset' [1] discusses the idea of the 'fixed' and 'growth' mindset.

---

1. Mindset: The New Psychology of Success by Carol Dweck, Robinson Publishing

A Fixed Mindset

A fixed mindset refers to a belief that abilities, intelligence, and talents are static and unchangeable traits. Individuals with a fixed mindset tend to believe that their skills and qualities are innate and cannot be significantly developed through effort or learning. This mindset can limit personal growth, resilience, and adaptability, as individuals may avoid challenges or give up easily in the face of setbacks.

Here are some examples of how a fixed mindset manifests in the real world:

Avoidance Of Challenges:

Individuals with a fixed mindset may avoid taking on new challenges or pursuing opportunities for growth because they fear failure. They may believe that failure reflects their inherent lack of ability and see it as a threat to their self-image.

Limited Persistence:

People with a fixed mindset may give up quickly when faced with obstacles or setbacks because they believe their abilities are fixed and cannot be improved through effort. They may lack the resilience and perseverance needed to overcome challenges.

Negative Feedback Response:

Individuals with a fixed mindset may react defensively to criticism or feedback, viewing it as a personal attack on their abilities rather than an opportunity for growth. They may become discouraged or disheartened by constructive feedback and may be less likely to seek out opportunities for improvement.

Comparison And Judgement:

Fixed mindset individuals may engage in frequent comparison with others and judgement of their abilities. They may view the success of others as a reflection of innate talent rather than effort, leading to feelings of envy or inadequacy.

It is likely that the Always-Right Autocrat does suffer from a fixed mindset.

A fixed mindset is not a permanent state and can be shifted with effort and self-awareness. By cultivating a growth mindset—belief in one's ability to learn and grow through effort and perseverance—individuals can overcome the limitations imposed by a fixed mindset and unlock their full potential for growth and development.

The 'growth' mindset links effort to outcome i.e. "If I revise, then I will achieve success in the exam." "If I go to the gym every day, I am more likely to be on the winning side in the football match."

The problem with the 'fixed' mindset is that it is so tied to the sense of identity. If the child does not do well in the mathematics test, then are they still 'good at maths?'

If I lose the tennis match does this mean I am still 'good at tennis?'

Those with a 'fixed' mindset of "I am intelligent and skilled." may also add a belief that "I am always right."

Any challenges to this are a challenge to the identity itself.

We all like to be right. Many of us will accept, however, there may be information of which we are unaware. When this is added into the mix we are often prepared to change or modify our view. The Always-Right Autocrats cannot do this. Their need to be right is so ingrained that they experience psychological pain when someone challenges their view.

When arguing with one of these people you may find they resort to techniques such as:

- Twisting the facts
- Re-interpreting the information presented
- Finding obscure loopholes in your argument
- Focusing on irrelevant parts of the argument
- Making personal attacks
- Outright denials
- Bold face lying

It can make for very unpleasant interactions.

The Golden Rule For Dealing With Always-Right Autocrats

Don't try to prove they are wrong.

There is a story of the wind and the sun having an argument about who is stronger.

To settle the argument, they look down on the Earth and see a man wearing a hat, walking along the street.

They agree to settle the argument with a competition. Whoever can get the hat off the man's head will be declared the strongest.

The wind agrees to go first. The wind blows and blows. The man pulls his hat tight onto his head. The wind blows harder, and the man holds his hat tighter. No matter how hard the wind blows, the man just holds his hat tightly to his head.

Eventually the wind gives up and allows the sun to have a turn.

The sun beats hotter and hotter and in a short time the man takes off his hat to use as a fan on his face.

The moral of the story?

You won't solve every problem with force.

The more you try to prove the Always-Right Autocrat is wrong, the more they will dig into their position and refuse to move.

This won't work.

It doesn't matter that they are wrong. Even if you could prove it without any doubt they would still deny it and probably change direction to prove you wrong on something else.

So How Do You Deal With An Always-Right Autocrat?

If playing to win will not work, then you could play to draw.

Assertive people work on the principle of trying to meet as many of their own and as many of the interests of the other person as possible.

This means there is no compulsion to pursue a win/lose strategy.

You will pursue a win/win strategy instead.

This means putting forward your views, ideas, and opinions without trampling over those of the other.

When you are in a conversation with your Always-Right Autocrat you can work to accept their point of view.

It doesn't mean you have to accept it in its entirety.

You need to ensure that your approach:

- Respects their view (without explicitly agreeing with it)
- Demonstrates that you have listened to their view and have considered it
- Gives no indication you are dismissive of their view
- Puts forward your own view
- Opens the door to further discussion

OR

- Closes the door to further discussion without putting them down or indicating they are wrong

Example 1:

“That is a very interesting idea. I hadn’t thought about it that way. Let’s make that one of the ideas we consider further. What other ideas could we also put on the list?”

The Always-Right Autocrat may say, “We don’t need any other ideas. This is the right one.” but you will stick to your guns and repeat what you just said. “Yes I agree it is one of the ideas we should consider. But let’s keep our options as open as possible. What other ideas might we consider?”

When it comes to making your choice, you can revisit the objective criteria for making your choice. Does their idea fulfill all the necessary criteria better than the other ideas you have put forward?

If it does not, you can ask the other person to question why this is their preferred solution.

Example 2:

"You make some interesting points. I have looked at it in a slightly different way. Let me share some of my thoughts and see if we can come up with a solution that works for both of us."

If the other person says, "I don't need to hear your thoughts. My ideas are all we need to consider." they are exposing themselves as uninterested in the views of others. This leaves you free to explain that if the other person doesn't even want to hear your ideas, there is no point in you being part of the conversation.

Whilst that last example can feel a little harsh it is important to note that win/win is not the same as win/lose.

Many people tell me that they have tried win/win, and it does not work.

When I ask why it didn't work, they reply, "Because I lost, and the other side won."

This is not win/win.

In any discussion you are entitled to your views, your thoughts,and your opinions. If the other person is entitled to forcefully put forward their views then so are you. If they are not prepared to listen to your views, why should you listen to theirs?

So In Summary...

When dealing with the Always-Right Autocrat do not play for a win/lose outcome. Play for the win/win outcome.

Chapter 12

The Jeering Jester

Humour is a wonderful thing. It is often said that laughter is the best medicine.

There are claims that when we laugh:

- We burn calories
- We release Endorphins that make us feel good
- We relax
- We boost our immune system
- Our stress levels reduce
- Blood pressure lowers

This is all wonderful but sometimes humour can be corrupted and weaponised.

You may encounter people with a cruel sense of humour.

When they make jokes it is often at the expense of others, how they look, how they dress, how they speak, how they act.

If you make a suggestion they will ridicule it with sarcasm, or absurdity.

The intention is to make others in the room laugh and destroy your idea.

If you get upset or offended by the ridicule their answer is likely to be, “What’s the matter, can’t you take a joke?”

Then they try to paint you as a killjoy or lacking a sense of humour.

Humorous people often learn this strategy in childhood.

There are two major ways in which people often use humour in everyday situations:

As A Defence Mechanism

Children who were most at risk of being bullied for whatever reason, or children who struggled academically at school, may have adopted humour as a defence mechanism.

If the other children, including the bullies, were laughing at them, they were safe.

Many comedians write in their autobiographies that they learned to be funny at school for exactly this reason.

If they were not academically gifted, they could still charm the teachers and adults around them by making them laugh.

These types of people are not normally cruel with their humour. They use it as a defence mechanism not a control mechanism.

Their humour is more likely to be kind and good-hearted and genuinely funny.

As A Control Mechanism

Some people learn that humour can be used to control others. By ridiculing one person, they send a message to others that the same fate can befall them if they dare to incur the displeasure of the bully.

If one of their acolytes fails to laugh at the bully's joke there will be consequences.

As these people get older, they learn to master the arts of cynicism, sarcasm, and ridicule.

For the targets of this humour it can be very unpleasant.

Having your idea being dismissed is bad enough but having people laugh at you at the same time appears far worse. If you dare to try to fight back, you will be dismissed as a misery who just doesn't get the joke.

In some ways, these people have much in common with the Always-Right Autocrat in that a stupid idea to them must also be a stupid idea to others.

It would be worthless to point out to them that you could ridicule most great ideas if you really tried.

Imagine, in the early days of the career of the great Lord Andrew Lloyd Webber, people asking him about his next shows. As Lord Lloyd Webber outlined the subject of his first few musicals, imagine the sarcastic response of the Jeering Jester

"You're going to do a musical based on Old Possum's Book of Cats? What are you going do...are you going to have everybody dressed as a cat?" (The acolytes laugh hysterically)

"You're going to do a musical based on Thomas the Tank Engine. How are you going to do the trains? You're not seriously going to put everybody on roller skates?" (The acolytes laugh hysterically)

"You're going to do a musical about Eva Peron, the wife of an Argentinian President? Well good luck with that. It sounds riveting." (The acolytes laugh hysterically)

Of course we all now know that Cats, Starlight Express and Evita went on to achieve enormous international success.

Any of us could ridicule anything if we really wanted, but it doesn't make us right.

How Do You Deal With The Jeering Jester?

The golden rule here is:

Don't engage with the joke

You may feel the need to appease them by laughing along but, if their joke has upset you, do not engage.

If you engage you have validated the Jeering Jester. It can't have been such a bad comment if even the victim laughed.

Humour is easily killed. If a comedian tells a joke and no one laughs, it is the comedian who looks stupid, not the audience.

If it is a conversation where the only people present are you and the Jeering Jester your lack of response will be very powerful.

Admittedly this is harder if the Jeering Jester has an adoring audience who are all laughing hysterically. Even here you should not engage with the joke.

You may face further ridicule when you fail to laugh or even smile with sarcastic comments such as, "Ooh he didn't find that funny." (Jester awaits further laughter from the crowd) or, "Ooh someone has had a humour bypass this morning."

Your deadpan lack of response will still speak volumes for you.

The Jester will feel awkward that you are not joining in with the jollity. More importantly, other people present will perceive your discomfort and may start to feel awkward for laughing in the first place.

Most people are not bullies or unkind.

The 'pack' mentality can be quite powerful, and we can all get carried away in the moment. Your lack of response may be the first step to bringing us back to recognising the nature of the bullying that is being used here.

It is likely the Jeering Jester may use the age old, "What's the matter, can't you take a joke?"

The correct response here is to say in as neutral a tone as you can manage, "I didn't find that funny."

It is an 'I' statement. There is no counter-attack on the Jeering Jester and it will send a powerful signal to those around you that, if they laugh at this, the audience is as guilty as the Jester in causing your distress.

Sometimes, if the Jeering Jester is using ridicule and sarcasm to dismiss your ideas, it may be best to ignore the sarcastic tone completely and to stare them out.

If we went back to our Andrew Lloyd Webber example about Starlight Express

Let's imagine the Jester said in a sarcastic tone,

"How are you going to do the trains. Are you going to put everyone on roller skates?"

Your response was,

"Yes." You say no more and no less. Put the ball back in their corner and await their response.

If they say, "Well that's just ridiculous." you might say something like, "I disagree."

Don't give explanations or justifications until the Jester has finished their little performance.

Eventually somebody is likely to say, "Can we just explore this roller skates idea a little more?"

In Summary...

Humour is supposed to be funny. If you find it hurtful, offensive,or upsetting then it is not funny to you. You have a right to express that. It is not your obligation to say why you don't find it funny. It is enough that you don't.

Chapter 13

Double-Dealing Deceivers

This melodramatic title refers to those who say one thing to your face and another behind your back.

Sometimes these people don't mean to be malicious. They may be 'people pleasers' and say what others wish to hear. Consequently, their opinion depends largely upon the last person they spoke to.

When they talked to you about your project, they may genuinely have felt it was a good idea. When they spoke to your colleague, who hated your project, the people-pleaser may have found themselves agreeing. They may even feel guilty about this and try to minimise the discrepancy at a later date after they have had time to think.

Other Double-Dealing Deceivers are more deliberate in their deception. (Try saying that sentence six times fast!). These people like to manipulate and play politics.

Shakespeare described such people in the character of Iago in the play 'Othello'

Iago knew how to influence Othello to believe Othello's wife was being unfaithful to him. Iago didn't say it directly. He often pretended to be Desdemona's ally, whilst dripping his poison into her husband's ear.

Double-Dealing Deceivers of this type are dangerous. Their behaviour is almost always to benefit them and hurt you.

You may not even realise they are your enemy. After all, they are so nice to your face.

How Do You Deal With The Double-Dealing Deceivers?

In his book 'Blink' Malcom Gladwell[1] describes how human beings are able to use senses honed over hundreds of thousands of years to assess a situation almost in the blink of an eye.

Undoubtedly this is a survival mechanism.

Our ancestors needed to assess danger extremely quickly. When we emerged from our cave, our primitive brain would have registered danger very quickly. Only when we got back into the safety of the cave would our neocortex have registered there was a different smell in the air, an

1. Blink: The Power of Thinking Without Thinking By Malcolm Gladwell - Penguin

unusual noise in the undergrowth or a movement in the bushes.

Human beings are able to assess danger quite accurately. We may have become a little desensitised to this early warning system in modern times, but it is still there.

When we encounter the Double-Dealing Deceiver it is important to trust our instincts.

Did you ever meet someone and, almost from the first seconds of meeting them, you made up your mind that this person was not to be trusted? If questioned, you would find it hard to pinpoint why you mistrusted this individual but that doesn't alter the fact the mistrust is registered.

Were you proven right later?

It might have been days, weeks, months or years later when the mistrusted person did something that absolutely confirmed the impression reached within nano-seconds of meeting them.

Our instincts should not be ignored.

This does not mean we should be overwhelmed by our biases and prejudices. The adage 'do not judge a book by its cover' is equally valid.

There are some people who give a bad first impression and go on to become your firm friends.

If, however, every fibre of your being is telling you not to trust the person in front of you, then listen.

Do Not Let It Hide In The Shadows

Double-Dealing Deceivers operate best in secret. It serves their purpose if the parties involved do not communicate with each other.

If you become aware of backstabbing or troublemaking behaviour, you need to bring it into the open.

Be careful how you address this.

It may be tempting to address it directly with words like "You are a liar." or "I can't trust a word you say." but this is likely to escalate the situation in unpredictable ways.

It is unlikely the Deceiver is going to admit their wrongdoing. More likely they will deny it, try to cast you as the villain and/or justify their own behaviour.

A direct attack is likely to make them dig into their own positions.

There are more effective ways to address this.

Step 1.

Let the Deceiver know you know they have been giving different messages to other people e.g.

"You told me you wanted to be involved in the project, but Mary told me you said you weren't interested in the project."

Keep it factual and report only what was said. Do not elaborate beyond the words Mary actually used. If you start interpreting or embellishing what Mary said, then you are as guilty of talking behind someone's back as the Deceiver.

Step 2.

Explain how this makes you feel.

You might find the following phrases useful:

"I don't understand."

Or

"I'm confused."

These phrases allow the other person to save face with no hint of an attack or accusation from you.

Step 3.

Invite them to explain with a phrase like

"Can you help me to understand please? What is the real situation?"

Or

"Can you help clear up the confusion. How do you see the project now?"

You have made it clear that you are aware of the double-dealing.

You have made no accusation.

You have invited an explanation.

If the Double-Dealer was behaving badly at least they are now aware that you are aware of their actions. They will be more wary of trying this again with you.

If they were not deliberately being malicious and it was just misguided behaviour they will appreciate that you did not try to humiliate or expose them and they are likely to be more careful in the future.

What If It Keeps Happening?

You can try the approaches described above a few times. Each time you do it you reinforce that you are not fooled or deceived.

If the behaviour does continue more than a couple of times after trying this, you can try a different approach.

When you are in a discussion with the Double-Dealer and you reach an agreement i.e "So we are agreed we will do that?" and the response is "Yes I agree."

You can be quite direct and say something like:

"I have heard you agree with me before and then say something different to someone else. How do I know it will be different this time?"

You might ask them to send you an email to confirm the agreement – that way you have it in writing.

Or you could work on the basis they will betray you and it will be a pleasant surprise if they do not.

You could organise yourself, so you do not need to work or cooperate with this person any more.

There is no one approach that will work every time but a combination of one or more of these may be of use.

Chapter 14

Scornful Snipers

These are a variation of the Jeering Jesters. They are masters of sarcasm and are completely dismissive of anybody's ideas other than their own. They are, however, often humourless in their dismissal of other people's ideas.

They are big fans of the 'not-invented-here syndrome'. If the Scornful Sniper did not originate the idea, then it can't be very good.

They will be dismissive of any new strategy or policy introduced by their company or manager.

They are contemptuous of any attempt by their friends or partners to make any improvements in their lives.

In the 1980's, comedian Harry Enfield created a character who summed up the Scornful Sniper. The character took the form of an elderly relative who, whenever he saw friends or relatives attempting something, would often say, "You don't want to do it like that."

Why Do They Behave In This Way?

There is often a huge element of fear behind this behaviour.

When a new policy or strategy is introduced, the Scornful Sniper may experience a minor panic attack. They may ask themselves:

- What if I don't understand the new policy?
- What if I can't implement it or make it work?
- What if others are better at the new strategy than me?
- Could this lead to me losing my job?

System 1 and the primitive brain are in full flow here.

This primitive response goes back to a basic survival instinct.

If you lived in a cave and one day you emerged from your cave to find two bushes had bloomed with juicy berries. One bush contains berries you and your tribe had eaten many times before. You know the fruit is delicious and safe.

The other bush contains berries you have never seen before. If you eat them, you may die. No matter how juicy the new berries look, your instinct will be to dismiss them in favour of the berries you normally eat.

This makes a great deal of sense when it comes to things that may kill you. Unfortunately, this instinct can become the driving force in many of us and lead us to become highly resistant to change of any kind.

When a new policy or strategy is introduced, our primitive brain responds by asking, "Could this kill me?"

It may not be a literal death, but the end of one's career, job or comfortable way of life is enough to resist the policy at all costs.

It is no different when it comes to relationships.

Some Scornful Snipers can be monsters to their partners. If their partner wants to lose weight, dress differently, get a new qualification or even broaden their social circle, the Sniper may go into overdrive.

This time the Sniper may be asking themselves:

- What if it changes the person you are?
- What if I don't like the person you become?
- What if the change means you will no longer like me?
- What if you leave me?

Fear and insecurity can be enormous drivers of sniping behaviour.

Some people can fall into the low benchmark trap.

This involves believing that 'for me to be successful everyone around me must fail.'

In some cases, they are worried about trying new things for themselves. They are afraid to pursue new avenues, new ideas, new strategies or pursue their ambitions. They can live with this as long as the people around them are not seen to be successfully pursuing their own ambitions.

If those around them are seen to be successful it serves to heighten the sense of personal failure in the Scornful Sniper. It becomes unbearable for them.

This means when responding to others:

- All achievements must be diminished
- All ambitions must be ridiculed as impossible or unrealistic
- All suggestions must be dismissed
- All changes must be challenged

Becoming Resilient

If you are unlucky enough to work with or be in a relationship with a Scornful Sniper, understanding their behaviour may be helpful in controlling your response to them. Be careful, however, that their behaviour does not do long-term damage to you.

Self-image and self-confidence are fragile commodities for most of us. It is destabilising when someone close to us criticises and demolishes every idea, dream or ambition we have.

According to legend, Thomas Edison made thousands of prototypes of the light bulb before he finally got it right. The Scornful Sniper would undoubtedly have ridiculed Edison and insisted he was wasting his time.

Imagine if the Scornful Sniper had seen the author J.K. Rowling, typing out a book about a boy wizard instead of getting a 'proper' job. What would the Scornful Sniper have said to the author who had just become divorced, was on social benefits, and could barely afford food for her or her baby?

In the mind of the Sniper, they are right, reasonable, sensible and will often say words like, "I am only trying to help." "You need to face reality." "There is no point in having your head in the clouds."

The problem with this is that nobody knows.

Nobody could predict with accuracy that Edison would eventually succeed with the electric light bulb. Nobody could predict Harry Potter would conquer the world. All the odds were against them.

That didn't stop Edison from inventing the electric light bulb and Harry Potter changing the reading habits of millions of people worldwide.

Your dreams may fail. You may not realise your ambitions, but it is not up to the Scornful Sniper to decide whether or not you should pursue them. It is up to you.

Even if they are experts, it doesn't mean they are automatically correct.

Singer Mika was rejected by Simon Cowell before landing a highly successful record deal.

Richard Paul Rowe was Head of A&R (Singles) at Decca Records from the 1950s to the 1970s. He is reputed to be the man who did not sign the Beatles.

Even experts can be wrong.

Resilience is the ability to adapt and persevere when things do not go as planned or the odds are against us. Resilient people do not dwell on failures or give up; they acknowledge what has happened, learn from their mistakes, and work out how to move forward.

There are many factors that can influence resilience including:

- Personality
- Education
- Emotional intelligence
- Physical fitness
- Diet
- Exercise

Most of these will affect your self-confidence and self-image. If you feel good about yourself, you are more likely to be able to resist the attacks of the Scornful Sniper.

Author Fay Weldon wrote about this in her book 'The Life And Loves Of A She Devil'[1] This is a story about an unattractive woman whose husband leaves her for his attractive and successful lover. Rather than collapse and give in, the spurned wife works to gain qualifications, changes her physical appearance and eventually overcomes both her husband and his lover. She builds her resilience through her mental and physical efforts.

How To Respond To The Scornful Sniper

Believe In Yourself

If you don't believe in your ideas, strategies, policies, ambitions, ideas etc. then no one else will.

It is nicer when colleagues and friends and family support your ideas but there is no obligation on them to do so. Even when someone is attacking your ideas, it is important to keep in mind what led you to make the decision or come up with the idea in the first place.

Listen But Do Not Be Led

By all means listen to what the Sniper is saying. But listen as objectively as you can.

Why are they saying these things? Does it come from jealousy, envy or fear? Is there any merit in any part of what they are saying? Can you take any of what they are saying and use it to improve your idea? Maybe they have pointed out something you had not considered.

Thank Them For Their Comments

You do not need to create unnecessary conflict. If the Sniper really believes they are trying to help you (and some of them really do believe that) you will not help the situation by attacking them.

Thank them for their comments and say they have given you something to think about.

Explain What You Are Going To Do

If you would like to incorporate any of their ideas into your plans, you can explain that you will do so. If you are not planning to use any of their suggestions or to change your plans you can say this too. You might say something like, "I value your comments and understand the points you are making but still feel my original plan is the path I want to take. And I will be taking that path."

If the Scornful Sniper persists then you will need to be strong.

Easier said than done, I know.

No matter how much the Scornful Sniper believes they are right, (and they may be right), only you are responsible for the decisions you make.

Here is the real problem with following the advice or recommendations of the Scornful Sniper.

If you follow their advice and they are wrong, their answer is often, "Well, I don't know why you listened to me. You should have trusted yourself. I was only offering a suggestion."

It is so easy for them to back off and downplay their role in your failure. After all, they don't have to live with the consequences of their failed advice. You do.

This is my main reason for maintaining control of the decisions I make.

I am prepared to listen to others and will try to keep an open mind to take on board sensible suggestions. Sometimes I receive a suggestion or recommendation that is so clear cut I would be foolish to ignore it. But occasionally I receive advice where it is not so clear cut as to what is the correct path.

On these occasions I take full responsibility for the decisions. Whatever other people may think, I am the one who has to live with the consequences of any decisions I make. Therefore, if I go against the advice of the Scornful Sniper and face taunts of, "Why are you ignoring my sensible advice?" "Why don't you follow my suggestions?" my answer is, "I need to live with the consequences of my decision right or wrong. I cannot expect you to take that responsibility. Therefore, I will make the decision. Even if it is not what you recommend, I will take full responsibility for it either way."

Whatever happens, at least you will have the satisfaction of knowing it was your decision rather than the foolishness of following advice from the Scornful Sniper. Advice that, in all probability, was advice with which you did not agree.

It is worth remembering the words of Marcus Aurelius

"It never ceases to amaze me: we all love ourselves more than other people, but care more about their opinion than our own."— **Marcus Aurelius,**

Chapter 15

Moaning Monsters

In every workplace, family, and social circle, there always seem to be people who constantly complain and find fault with everything. These people, whom we refer to as "Moaning Monsters" can drain your energy and make it challenging to work or live with them.

Energy and enthusiasm are contagious. As a trainer and presenter, I know that the energy in the room comes from the person at the front. If the presenter has lots of energy and enthusiasm, there is a good chance so will the rest of the room. Sadly, the reverse is also true. A negative person can suck all the energy from the room and the people within it.

You may have experienced this when you were at school. Some teachers could make even the most uninteresting subjects fascinating. Others appeared bored and miserable, and the lessons seemed interminable as a result.

The same can happen at work. One miserable and negative team member can affect the mood of the entire department.

However, there are ways to handle these individuals that can help you maintain your sanity and even improve your relationship with them. In this chapter, we will explore strategies for dealing with Moaning Monsters.

Characteristics Of The Moaning Monster

- They always look for the negative in every situation
- Nothing is ever going to work
- Everybody else is an idiot and against them

They will often start their sentences with:

- We tried that before and it didn't work...
- Yes but...
- That won't work here...
- The problem is...
- I can't see how that will help...
- You don't understand the difficulties we are facing...

Why Do They Behave Like This?

It is essential to understand why some people complain and are negative all the time. In some cases, negative behaviour may stem from underlying issues such as stress, anxiety, or depression. Sometimes, people may be going through a tough time in their personal lives, and their negativity is a coping mechanism. Therefore, you may need to show empathy and compassion towards the individual.

You Don't Always Know What Goes On Behind Closed Doors

We are not always the people we want to be.

In his wonderful book 'A Christmas Carol'[1] Charles Dickens tells us of Ebeneezer Scrooge. Whilst the popular image is of the elderly miser, the book describes Scrooge as a lonely schoolboy, as having once having been in love, as a loyal and enthusiastic apprentice to Fezziwig and as an enterprising entrepreneur with his partner Jacob Marley. But somewhere along the line Scrooge lost his way and forgot who he really was. It takes the ghosts of Christmas past, present and future to remind him.

In some ways we can all be like this. We may not have grown up to be the people we wanted to be.

Life takes its toll. Each disappointment, failure and disaster leave their mark upon us.

Although life is hard for all of us, some people face more hardship and difficulty than others. Don't assume you know what is going on in someone else's life.

Some people are suffering from problematic marriages or relationships where each day is like a constant battle.

---

1. A Christmas Carol by Charles Dickens, Oxford University Press

Others have illnesses themselves that may not be visible to you, or they may be providing care to sick partners, parents, children, siblings or grandchildren. Others may be facing financial difficulties, nightmare neighbours or self-esteem issues from horrific childhoods.

As much as we may say, "You should not bring your problems to work." we are not robots and we do carry with us our emotional baggage.

If you had had a massive row with your partner just before leaving for work, do you really think you would not dwell on it for the whole day?

If you had a child with special needs or a sick parent at home, do you really think you would be able to forget them between the hours of 9 a.m. and 5 p.m. when at work?

The point is that the Moaning Monster may be suffering a great deal of pain that they cannot necessarily express at home. They may feel that work is the only place they can really express their frustrations and agonies. It's not right and they should not do that, but sometimes we cannot help ourselves.

Don't assume their negativity is always aimed at you or caused by you.

If you respond to this negativity by taking it personally you are likely to inflame the situation.

The Vicious Circle

One cause of the negativity that can affect us is negativity itself.

As we feel a little down, or experience an upset that throws us off balance, it can begin an escalating spiral. We get upset by one thing and we then react more negatively to the next which, in turn, makes us more negative to the next thing that arises and so on.

Suddenly our first response to everything becomes negative. We hate the world and everyone in it. This can be caused or made worse by things such as watching, listening to, or reading the daily news.

George Orwell, in his book 'Nineteen Eighty-Four'[2], wrote about people observing the two-minute hate each day. They were shown pictures of the enemy and urged to scream, shout and rant at the image.

It feels to me that modern news programmes are the equivalent of Orwell's two-minute hate. We are presented with news articles about the government and the failure of the economy and practically urged to scream abuse at those on screen. It is guaranteed to leave us feeling negative at the end of the programme.

Social media can also play a part in this.

---

2. Nineteen Eighty-Four by George Orwell, Penguin Publishers

“Doomscrolling" is a term used to describe the act of obsessively consuming negative news on social media or other digital platforms, often to the point of feeling overwhelmed or distressed. It refers to the tendency of people to scroll endlessly through their feeds, seeking out news and information about disasters, crises, and other negative events. The term "doomscrolling" became more prevalent during the COVID-19 pandemic, as people spent more time online and were exposed to a constant stream of news about the pandemic, as well as other global crises. Doomscrolling can have negative effects on mental health and well-being, as it can lead to feelings of anxiety, helplessness, and despair. It is important to take breaks from social media and to limit the amount of negative news that one consumes to maintain a healthy and balanced perspective on the world.

Digesting too much negative media of any kind can have the same effect. Watching too many documentaries about how the world is ending, or atrocities committed through history, or even an endless diet of soap operas with their never-ending cycles of domestic abuse, adultery and even murder may leave their mark.

In the case of documentaries, it is good to be informed. The danger happens when this is overdone. Everything in moderation is good advice here. Watch some apocalyptic documentaries and some soap operas but try to balance it with the occasional comedy.

Moaning Monsters tend to have a low tolerance for frustration, making them more likely to complain about minor issues. They may also use complaining to seek attention or sympathy from others. Some Moaning Monsters may not even realise they are complaining and view their behaviour as merely expressing their opinions or thoughts.

Negativity can become a habit. We begin to normalise moaning and complaining as the most appropriate response to any situation.

In the UK complaining about the weather is a common conversation starter.

Visitors to the UK often find it strange that we are so obsessed with the weather. The thing about the UK weather is that it is highly changeable from month to month. From week to week, from day to day and even hour by hour. The UK population is largely happy in a temperature between 12 and 24 degrees Celsius. Anything lower or higher becomes worthy of comment. Anything lower than 12 degrees will be greeted with cries of "It's too cold." Anything above 25 degrees and we will shout "It's too hot." If it rains for more than three days you will hear cries of "Is this rain ever going to end?" If it hasn't rained for a week you will hear "The gardens could do with some rain."

The point is that the weather gives us something to talk about.

In other countries (as well as the UK) you will hear debates about public transport, the state of the economy or the incompetence of the government. These subjects give us topics for conversation in which everyone can participate. Many people find it difficult to make conversation. General chit-chat is torture for them. "I never know what to say." is a common cry. Consequently, we often fall back into 'safe' subjects of general life irritants e.g. the cost of living or the poor state of healthcare.

The problem is that it can be hard to get out of this cycle once in it. We begin to moan and complain about everything, and we are not always aware we are doing it. The people around us are extremely aware and it can make us unpleasant without realising.

Strategies For Dealing With Moaning Monsters

Practice Empathy

Empathy is different from sympathy.

Empathy and sympathy are two related but distinct concepts that describe our emotional responses to the feelings and experiences of others.

Empathy is the ability to understand and share the feelings of others. It involves putting oneself in someone else's shoes and imagining what it would be like to experience their emotions, thoughts, and experiences. Empathy requires active listening and paying close attention to another person's words, tone of voice, and body language. It helps to build deeper connections and stronger relationships, as it shows we care about the feelings of others.

Sympathy, on the other hand, is the expression of concern or sorrow for someone else's situation. It is a feeling of compassion and understanding that arises when we recognise that someone is going through a difficult time. Sympathy does not necessarily require understanding or sharing the other person's emotions or experiences, but rather acknowledges their pain or suffering.

Sympathy can be tricky in that some people will confuse it with 'pity' and see it as patronising that you, a relative stranger, feel sorrow about their situation. Empathy is about ensuring you try to understand their challenges.

The first step in empathetically dealing with Moaning Monsters is to understand where they are coming from.

Try to put yourself in their shoes and understand why they might be feeling negative or complaining. Remember, you don't know what is going on in their life.

I once arrived early at a training course to set up. One of the participants was already there. I had met this person before and did not have a very positive view of her. She seemed to me to be a Moaning Monster. She never smiled or joined in any of the jokes and never responded very positively to anything we were doing.

As we were the only two people there, I asked her if she was looking forward to the weekend. "Not really." she replied, confirming my view of her. Then she began to explain that her partner had a terminal illness. As a result, he had had to leave work, which meant they were in financial distress and had had to move to a smaller apartment. She had a child and was facing the reality of becoming a single parent in the very near future as well as losing the person she loved.

My admiration for this person rose enormously. Not because she was going through these things, but because each day she still got into work and, by all accounts, did a good job when she was there. If that had been me, I suspect I would have been a quivering wreck sobbing in the corner of the room. Not really a surprise this person did not smile or laugh a lot.

We rarely know the struggles other people are facing.

One way to better understand those challenges is to use active listening skills. This involves listening attentively, asking clarifying questions, and summarising what the person is saying. This doesn't mean 'prying' into their personal affairs, but sometimes people just need to vocalise some of their challenges.

They don't need you to solve them or even to share their pain. Just listen attentively. By doing so, you can ensure you understand their perspective and make them feel heard. You may find that is what they really need.

Don't Take It Personally

It is crucial not to take their behaviour personally. Their negativity is often not directed towards you specifically, but it's a habit they may have developed over time. It is essential to maintain your composure, remain calm, and not get emotionally involved in their negativity.

Imagine you experience negative behaviour from someone serving you in a shop or a restaurant. The service is OK, but the person serving you does not smile, or seem particularly happy.

When somebody behaves negatively towards us, there is a huge temptation to respond in kind – to teach them a lesson and show them that we will not tolerate their negativity.

Sadly, the effect is often the opposite to that we intended.

If their negative behaviour is driven by problems at home or health-related issues, your negative response may be the final straw that just tips the person over the edge. The lesson they will learn is that life is truly awful and there are no glimmers of hope.

If the negative behaviour from the service provider is driven through habit and they are not even aware they are responding to everything negatively, your negative response may just confirm that the world is full of horrible people. This confirms to them there is no point in being nice. This becomes a vicious circle and only encourages them to be more negative.

Fight the temptation to take it personally. It is not all about you. Don't be part of the problem. Be part of the solution instead.

Encourage Positive Thinking

Moaning Monsters often struggle to see the positive side of situations, leading to a negative mindset. Encouraging positive thinking can help shift their perspective and make them more optimistic.

You might try behavioural conditioning. This is similar to the positive reinforcement we discussed for dealing with Bullies and Dominators.

Behavioural Conditioning, also known as classical conditioning or Pavlovian conditioning, is a type of learning in which a neutral stimulus is paired with a stimulus that naturally triggers a response, and over time, the neutral stimulus alone can elicit the same response. For example, if a person always eats a particular food and experiences pleasure, the sight or smell of that food can eventually trigger a pleasurable (conditioned) response, even in the absence of the food itself.

This process was first studied by Ivan Pavlov in the late 1800s, who famously conditioned dogs to salivate at the sound of a bell.

When it comes to dealing with Moaning Monsters we work on the basis that human beings need response. Almost all human behaviour is designed to get a response from others. When we tell a joke we want others to laugh. When we give instructions we want others to follow them. When we describe our problems we want others to empathise or sympathise or even modify their behaviour to meet our needs and wants.

Focus your response to their behaviour by responding more to positive comments and behaviour than to the negative.

You could also start by pointing out positive aspects of a situation or encouraging them to focus on what they are grateful for.

Another way to encourage positive thinking is to avoid negative self-talk. If you hear a Moaning Monster criticising themselves, you could try to redirect the conversation and encourage them to speak positively about themselves.

Encourage Solutions-Thinking

Moaning Monsters often complain without offering any solutions to the problems they have identified. As a result, it can be frustrating to listen to them. If you are a manager who has a team member who continually comes to you with problems, you may not have the solution or the time to try to find one. This can leave both you and the complainer feeling very unsatisfied.

For those people who have fallen into the vicious cycle of negativity you can play a part in breaking that cycle by listening to the problems they have raised and then asking them to take some time to work on, or identify potential solutions.

Human beings love solving problems. We are almost genetically encoded to solve problems. We are the greatest problems-solvers the world has ever known. Arguably we are also the greatest problem-causers the world has ever known. Problem-solving is what got us out of trees and out of caves in the first place.

Have you ever walked past someone doing a crossword puzzle or a jigsaw puzzle? The urge to join in or help solve some of the clues or add a few pieces is irresistible. If you can get your negative person into a problem-solving mode, you might also notice they become less emotional.

As we discussed in earlier chapters, the problem-solving function of the brain is less emotional than the problem identification function of the human brain because the former involves higher-level cognitive processes that are more analytical.

When we identify a problem, our brain is often influenced by our emotional reactions to the situation, which can bias our perception of the problem and make it difficult to think objectively. This in turn can make us feel frustrated, depressed, or unsatisfied. However, when we engage in problem-solving, we must use our cognitive processes to analyse the problem, evaluate possible solutions, and select the best course of action. This requires a more rational and analytical approach that is less affected by emotions.

The problem-solving function of the brain involves the neocortex, which is responsible for executive functions such as planning, decision-making, and problem-solving. This area of the brain, as we covered earlier, is less involved in emotional processing compared to other areas such as the amygdala, which is responsible for processing emotions and generating emotional responses.

Overall, therefore, the problem-solving function of the brain is less emotional than the problem identification function.

So, when the Moaning Monster starts to complain you can listen and then follow with questions such as:

"How do you think we might solve that problem?"

"What do you suggest we do about it?"

"How might we improve the situation or remove that obstacle?"

It is possible the negative person has spent so long in the vicious cycle that they can't immediately re-programme their brain to think more productively and positively. You may need to give them some time to reflect and process their thoughts.

You could say something like

"You have raised some interesting problems here. Can I ask you to take some time to think about how you/we might solve some of those problems? Let's schedule a meeting for the end of the week so we can discuss some of your ideas and suggestions and see if we can resolve some or all these problems."

Reframe The Situation

One effective way to deal with negative people is to help them to reframe the situation.

The meaning of any event depends on the frame we wrap around that event.

Imagine that today it is raining. Is that good or bad?

If you were having a picnic or a barbecue, then it would be bad. If you were a gardener who had just planted some vegetables or plants, you might welcome the rain as a good thing.

Whether you were a gardener or planning a barbecue will not affect the fact that it is still raining. In itself, the fact that it is raining is neither good nor bad. What affects your mood or feeling is the frame (the barbecue or the picnic) through which you interpret the event (the rain).

The frame may be chosen for us contextually. For example, if you were on holiday with your children, you might be more likely to arrange a picnic. If you had a large garden and it was the spring, you might be more likely to plant bulbs. In either case your interpretation of the rain would be dependent on these events.

Sometimes the frame we choose might be subconscious and habitual. If you were in a bad mood, depressed or down on your luck, you might be more tempted to put a negative frame around any event.

"It's raining. Of course it is. It always rains on me just to make my life worse".

In reality the rain has nothing to do with you and it is unlikely that any supernatural force has specifically targeted you to soak.

Sadly, our Moaning Monsters will often put a negative frame around the events in their lives.

If the food you ordered in the restaurant takes a long time to arrive it is because the staff hate you and are deliberately making you wait. If you are not invited to a work meeting it is because they are secretly plotting to get rid of you. If your manager delegates a task to you, it is because your manager is lazy and trying to dump their bad jobs onto you

To address this you may need to encourage the negative person to reframe and consider the event in a more positive light.

For example:

Is it possible the food in the restaurant is taking a long time to arrive because it is being freshly and carefully prepared?

Is it possible you have not been invited to the work meeting because your team members value your time and know that what you are doing is more important than their meeting?

Is it possible your manager is delegating tasks to you because your manager trusts you and wants to use these tasks to develop you further to enhance your career?

In other words, you are asking them to consider "What are the positive aspects of this situation?"

Beware Of Solving The Problems Yourself

If you are a successful person, in a senior position, or have a highly ambitious drive you may find it hard to resist simply offering the solutions yourself. We should always try to keep in mind that our solutions to someone else's problems rarely work. It is their problem and therefore the solution should also be theirs. The danger of offering your own solution is that if it doesn't work, the blame will also be yours. If you recommend a solution to the negative person, they may try it. If it doesn't work, they will come back to you and say, "I did what you said and it didn't work. It's not my fault. What else would you suggest?"

However, you can take the lead by offering possible options to address their issues.

When offering options, be mindful of your tone and delivery. It's essential to approach the situation with kindness and not come across as condescending or dismissive. You could start by asking if they are open to hearing your ideas and then provide potential solutions that could help them overcome their issues.

Try to offer several options and invite them to reflect on which, if any, might help. The choice must ultimately be theirs. You could also offer several options and invite them to take them away, develop them, add to them and then come back to you with their chosen solutions or solutions.

Be A Good Listener And Not An 'Enabler'

Sometimes, negative people are not looking for someone to solve their problems. They just want someone to listen. Be a good listener and give them your undivided attention. Let them vent their frustrations and show empathy towards them. It may not solve the problem, but it can make the individual feel heard and understood.

Obviously, you need to be careful with this. There is a fine line between being a good listener and an 'enabler'.

Empathetic listening involves understanding and acknowledging the emotions and feelings of the person speaking to you. It requires active listening, paying attention to the speaker's words, tone, and body language, and responding in a way that shows you understand and care about their experiences.

On the other hand, being an enabler of bad behaviour means that you allow or even encourage negative behaviours or habits to continue by supporting them, making excuses for them, or avoiding confronting them.

While empathetic listening can be helpful in creating a safe and supportive environment for someone to share their feelings and experiences, it can become enabling if the listener does not set boundaries or address unhealthy behaviour when necessary. It's important to empathise with someone while still holding them accountable for their actions and encouraging them to make positive changes.

Set And Maintain Boundaries

Whilst it's essential to be empathetic to Moaning Monsters, you may also need to set boundaries. If their complaining is taking a toll on your mental health, it's okay to limit your exposure to them. For example, you could politely let them know that you are unable to engage in conversations about negative topics or limit your interactions with them altogether.

Setting boundaries can also involve redirecting the conversation. Suppose a Moaning Monster starts complaining about a particular topic. You could try to shift the conversation to a more positive subject or provide a solution to the problem they are discussing. However, it is crucial to do this in a polite and respectful manner, so as not to make the situation worse. You can communicate your boundaries by saying something like, "I understand you are upset, but I don't feel there is any point in dwelling on the problem. Let's focus on finding a solution instead."

Encourage Them To Seek Help

We live in an age where it is more acceptable to talk about mental health. The pressures of modern life do weigh heavily on us all.

Negative behaviour can sometimes be a sign that the other person is struggling and in need of help.

A consistent change in behaviour could also be a cry for help

If you notice someone who is usually calm and collected becoming short-tempered, aggressive, or distant, it may be a sign of an underlying issue.

If these were accompanied by any or all of the following at work or at home you should pay particular attention:

1. Uncharacteristic mistakes or poor performance at work: If someone's work quality or productivity suddenly takes a dip, it may be because they are dealing with something difficult.

2. Frequent absences or tardiness: If a person is consistently late or absent, it may indicate they are struggling with something that is affecting their ability to be present.

3. Self-destructive behaviour: If a person is engaging in harmful behaviours, such as substance abuse or self-harm, it is a clear sign that they need help.

If you notice any of these signs, it's important to approach the person with empathy and concern. You can ask if everything is okay. If the other person is open to a discussion, you can offer support or resources if they need it. Be aware that not everyone will want to discuss their problems with you and you should not force the issue. Remember that it's not your responsibility to solve their problems, but you can offer a listening ear and be there to support them if they are open t your help.

If you suspect that an individual's negativity stems from an underlying issue such as depression or anxiety, and they have indicated they are open to help, you can encourage them to seek professional help. Offer to support them through the process and assure them that it is okay to ask for help.

Don't Engage In Gossip Or Negativity

When demonstrating empathy, please make sure you avoid engaging in gossip or negative conversations with Moaning Monsters.

There is a difference between empathising and agreeing.

Empathising means you can understand and relate to the emotions or feelings that someone is expressing, without necessarily agreeing with their point of view. Agreeing, on the other hand, means that you share the same opinion or perspective as the other person.

For example, if someone expresses frustration with the behaviour of one of their colleagues, a neighbour or their partner, empathising might involve acknowledging that the behaviour of the colleague, neighbour or partner can be challenging and time-consuming, and recognising the stress and pressure that can come with it. However, agreeing might involve saying that you agree with the Moaning Monster's assessment of the individual or that you hate them as well.

It can be tempting to demonstrate agreement to gain the confidence and approval of the negative person, which might not be true or helpful in the situation.

The problem is that the negative person may use your agreement to reinforce their own negative behaviour. In some cases, they may even cite your agreement to the other person. E.g. Imagine one of your colleagues was the Moaning Monster and to establish a connection you had agreed, instead of empathised, that the Monster had made a correct negative assessment of the behaviour of a supplier. In the next meeting between the Moaning Monster and the supplier, the Monster might say, "It's not just me that thinks you have behaved badly. My manager also agrees with me that you are a terrible supplier."

You don't really think the supplier is bad at all, but now you are caught in the middle of the conflict between the two. At some stage you may be forced to admit you lied to the negative person (which will do nothing for your future relationship) or you have to destroy your relationship with the supplier.

Even if the situation were not so extreme, agreeing with the Moaning Monster instead of emphasising can encourage them to continue on their negative spiral.

Empathising, on the other hand, can help to build trust and rapport with others by showing that you understand and respect their perspective, even if you may not agree with them. It also allows for a deeper understanding of someone's feelings and can help to facilitate better communication and problem-solving.

Chapter 16

Silent But Deadly

These are the people who have information but will not share it.

They may have various reasons for not sharing the information, such as a desire to maintain power or control. For them "knowledge is power". They may have a fear of consequences for sharing, a lack of trust in others, or simply a preference for privacy.

In their own mind they may not see this as negative or difficult behaviour. After all, they took the time and effort to acquire the information. The information is equally available to others if they take the same time and effort.

They may feel they have no duty or responsibility to share information with people who are too lazy to find it for themselves.

In some cases, this may be learned behaviour. Nobody helped them and they were encouraged by parents, teachers or others, that if you wanted to know something, it was your own responsibility to find it.

In most organisations, there is a level of interdependency. Large organisations are built on that concept. Nobody can know everything, but with everybody working together, a large organisation can collectively find all the required answers.

Employees who refuse to share information, however, disrupt this model and can cause damage to their own teams and those who depend upon them.

Such individuals may be seen as uncooperative or unhelpful, particularly in situations where sharing information is necessary for the success of a project or to resolve an issue. Their behaviour can also be seen as suspicious or manipulative, particularly if they appear to be selectively sharing information with certain individuals but not others.

We call these people 'Silent But Deadly' not because they are literal murderers but because they can cause a lot of damage.

Their refusal to share information can be deadly to:

- Cooperation
- Communication
- Teamworking
- Productivity
- Trust

Overall, people who withhold information can create barriers to communication and collaboration, and may damage trust and relationships with others. It is important for individuals to consider the impact of their actions and to communicate openly and honestly in situations where information sharing is necessary.

How Do You Get Silent But Deadly To Share Information?

The simplest route to obtaining information is to ask for it.

This sounds like common sense and seemingly pointless with people who refuse to share information, but you need to ask yourself, "Is the reason they are not sharing information because I am not asking the right questions?"

You need to examine whether your questions are open-ended or closed-ended.

Remember that closed-ended questions are questions that can often be answered with a simple "yes" or "no", or a specific piece of information. They are often used to gather specific facts or to confirm or deny something.

Closed-ended questions are not always answered with a “yes” or “no” but it is possible to answer them in this way.

The problem with the Silent But Deadly people is that they will use your closed-ended question as an excuse to answer only the question they are asked.

You asked a closed-ended question, and you got only a “yes” or “no” in response. So, whose fault is that? Your choice of question gave them an excuse to withhold information.

Open-ended questions are questions that allow for a broad range of answers and require more than just a "yes" or "no" response.

With your Silent But Deadly people who are reluctant to share information it is vital we encourage them to speak with us. Until we can encourage them to share information, we cannot blame them for not sharing.

Getting people who are reluctant to share information to open up can be a challenging task, but, in addition to asking open-ended questions, here are a few more strategies that you can try:

Establish Trust

Sometimes the reason the information is not shared is that the other person does not trust you or what you will do with that information. Maybe they feel you will steal the credit for their ideas. Building trust is crucial to getting people to share information. Try to establish a personal connection with the person. Demonstrate that you are genuinely interested in their work and opinions and that they will receive full credit for their work and ideas. Remember that trust comes in on foot and gallops away on horseback. In other words, it can take a long time to build trust but seconds to destroy it. If your colleagues do share information with you, take the responsibility to handle that information with care. The first time you betray their trust may be the last time they ever share information with you.

Explain The Importance

I was once with a group of salespeople, talking about the importance of open-ended questions. Suddenly one of the participants on the course said, “But you don’t understand. Our clients don’t like to share information.” All the other participants nodded in agreement until one of the senior participants said, “But that’s not true.” The others looked at her as she added, “It is true that our clients will not share information to help our company, or to help the sales team, or to help the government. But they will share whatever information they need to share if they can see how that information will be of help to themselves.” Once again all the other participants nodded in agreement.

This is not just true of clients; it is probably true of most of us. There are many individuals and companies who ask us questions to find out more about us. Most of the time we treat them with suspicion because we don’t know how they are going to use the information we provide.

If you want people to share information with you, it is a good idea to help them understand why sharing information is essential for the team or organisation's success. Explain how their knowledge and insights can benefit others and contribute to achieving common goals. And explain what you will do with the information they have shared.

Create A Safe Space

People may be hesitant to share information if they feel judged or criticised. Even humour in the form of laughing at someone's ideas, or jokingly calling their ideas stupid or crazy can deter people from sharing information. You may only have meant it as a joke but that doesn't help someone with insecurities. Ensure everyone feels comfortable and respected and emphasise that all opinions and ideas are welcome. Then, when they do share their ideas, treat both the individual and their information with respect, even if you don't agree with them.

Incentivise Sharing

Consider offering incentives for sharing information, such as recognition or bonuses. Some organisations have set up suggestion schemes and rewarded employees for the value of their ideas if implemented. You could also provide opportunities for growth and development. If the information shared would be worth passing on to senior management, you might consider allowing the individual who gave you the information to present it themselves to the senior management.

Lead By Example

Do you share information openly and regularly yourself? Many managers find it difficult to share information openly. It may be they are not at liberty to share everything, but that can soon translate into 'share nothing'.

You cannot criticise your team for not sharing information if you hold all your cards close to your chest.

Try to be as transparent as your organisation and the information will allow and encourage others to do the same. Modelling the behaviour you want to see can be a powerful way to influence others.

Remember that some people may have legitimate reasons for not sharing information, such as concerns about confidentiality or fear of retaliation. Be respectful and understanding of their perspectives, and work to address their concerns.

Chapter 17

Vocal Volunteers

The term "Vocal Volunteers" refers to individuals who volunteer to take on tasks and responsibilities within an organisation or team, but do not follow through on their commitments. These individuals may be enthusiastic and vocal in expressing their willingness to help, but when it comes time to act, they fail to deliver.

Vocal Volunteers can be frustrating for those who are relying on them to complete tasks, as they create false expectations and add additional stress to already busy schedules. They may cause delays, misunderstandings, and ultimately, hinder the progress of a project or initiative. It is also puzzling as to why these people will put themselves forward and volunteer for tasks they are not going to do.

Some Vocal Volunteers are 'people pleasers' who have a strong desire to please others and be liked by their colleagues and superiors. They may go out of their way to accommodate others, avoid conflict, and seek approval or validation from others. They have learned that to be valued by others you must seek to be as useful and helpful as possible. They have not, however, learned to equate the difference between saying you will do a thing and actually doing it. The instant gratification of the smiles and congratulations of others when the Vocal Volunteers put themselves forward is often the reward they seek. Then they will find excuses, or become absent, when the task is not completed.

While people pleasers can be valuable team members, their behaviour can also have negative consequences, such as:

1. Burnout: Overcommitting and taking on too much can lead to burnout and exhaustion. Vocal Volunteers don't always recognise that trying to keep everyone happy can have a detrimental effect on themselves.

2. Underperformance: People pleasers may not be able to complete tasks to the best of their ability if they are spread too thinly or trying to please everyone. Vocal Volunteers have not yet learned that saying "no" is not the worst answer we can give. The worst answer is to say "yes" and not do it.

To address the issue of people pleasing in the workplace, it is important to encourage open communication and create a culture that values honest feedback and constructive criticism. Encouraging individuals to set boundaries and prioritise their workload can also help prevent burnout and ensure that everyone is performing at their best. Additionally, providing training and support to help individuals build their confidence and assertiveness can be beneficial.

One possible explanation for Vocal Volunteers' behaviour is that they may feel pressured to say “yes” to requests for help, even if they do not have the time, skills, or motivation to fulfil them.

They may also overestimate their abilities or underestimate the complexity of the task at hand, leading them to commit to more than they can handle.

To address the issue of Vocal Volunteers, it is important to have clear communication about expectations and deadlines, and to hold individuals accountable for their commitments. Providing training and support may also help individuals feel more confident and prepared to take on tasks. Additionally, creating a culture of accountability and follow-through can encourage individuals to be more honest about their limitations and realistic about their ability to help.

Chapter 18

Psychopaths And Sociopaths

"But what if none of these techniques work on the person I have to deal with?"

It is hopefully rare, but you may encounter someone with whom none of the techniques in this book work. You have tried to be reasonable with them, you have tried to understand them, you have tried using logic, you have tried to achieve a win-win solution, but it just won't wash and you end up destroyed in most of your encounters with this person.

It is possible you may have been unfortunate enough to encounter somebody demonstrating the behaviours of a psychopath or sociopath.

"Sociopath" and "psychopath" are not official diagnoses in the Diagnostic and Statistical Manual Of Mental Disorders (DSM-5) , the most widely used guide for diagnosing mental health conditions.

Psychopathy falls under the category of an official diagnosis of antisocial personality disorder (ASPD)

Antisocial Personality Disorder (ASPD) is a mental health condition characterised by a persistent pattern of disregard for, and violation of, the rights of others. Individuals with ASPD often exhibit a lack of empathy, impulsivity, deceitfulness, and a disregard for societal norms and rules. They may engage in behaviours such as lying, manipulation, aggression, and a consistent disregard for the safety and well-being of others. This disorder typically manifests in early adulthood and can lead to significant interpersonal problems.

Sociopathy is not recognised as a clinical condition.

Despite the innumerable films and books about characters such as Hannibal Lecter from Thomas Harris' 'The Silence Of The Lambs' or Norman Bates from Robert Blochs' 'Psycho', etc. Most psychopaths and sociopaths are not killers.

But they can still cause a lot of damage.

It could be argued that the financial crash of 2008 was one of the greatest example of mass psychopathy in history, with a group of psychopaths operating in such a way that very nearly destroyed the economy of the whole world.

Whilst there may be areas of overlap between psychopathy and sociopathy, they do have distinct traits. According to Bhambhani, Prakash and Tripathi in their article: Psychopathy and sociopathy: A modern understanding of antisocial personality disorder, published in the Indian Journal of Social Studies and Humanities 2021:

The differences between a Sociopath and a Psychopath might be described as:

Traits Of A Sociopath:

- Breaking the law
- Physical aggression
- Manipulation of others for personal gain
- Anger and hostility
- Unpredictable mood swings
- Impulsive behaviours
- Chaotic and dramatic
- Exploitation of other people
- Irresponsibility
- Unreliable in relationships

Traits Of A Psychopath:

- Feeling few (if any) emotions
- Sadism (pleasure from causing pain to others)
- Lack of care for others
- Pathological lying
- Charming personality
- Lack of fear
- Risk-taking behaviour
- Inability to love
- No remorse for wrongdoing
- Poor judgement
- Lack of life goals
- Use relationships purely for gain

The causes of sociopathy are not well known, but it is generally thought that children brought up in violent or abusive environments are more likely to develop sociopathy.

Psychopathy is associated with a dysfunction of the amygdala. The amygdala is a critical brain structure involved in various aspects of:

- Emotional processing
- Fear conditioning
- Social and emotional behaviour
- Memory formation
- Stress response

The reason for including sociopaths and psychopaths in this book is that if you are unlucky enough to find yourself in a relationship with either, you may find few of the techniques described in the book will work.

This is very hard if the sociopath or psychopath is your boss it can be even harder if it is your romantic partner or a family member.

The reason why this can be so hard is the same reason it is difficult to treat sociopaths or psychopaths...they don't believe there is anything wrong with them. In other words, all the problems are caused by other people.

In addition, no medication can cure sociopathy or psychopathy. There is medication that may help manage some of the symptoms. Even therapy may be of limited use.

Where might we experience a psychopath?

It is estimated that 1% of the population are psychopaths

Those numbers rise exponentially in prison, where 15% to 25% of inmates show some of these characteristics.[1]

According to the Psychologia website, approximately 4% of the population are sociopaths.[2]

This is not to say that many more people don't have sociopathic or psychopathic traits.

According to Kevin Dutton, a British psychologist and writer, who specialises in the study of psychopathy these are the top 5 professions that attract psychopaths.[3]

In descending order:

- CEO
- Lawyer
- Media
- Salesperson
- Surgeon

It may seem alarming to see this list. If you work in any of these areas and you are thinking "But I'm not a psychopath." be assured it certainly doesn't mean ALL CEOs and lawyers etc. are psychopaths. It just means these professions attract a slightly larger than average percentage. Psychopaths like

---

1. Burton, B, & Saleh, F.M.,Psychiatric Times
2. https://psychologia.co/psychopath-vs-sociopath/
3. Dutton, Kevin, The Wisdom Of Psychopaths

power and these professions give them a lot of power. Of course they are attracted to these areas. But take a moment to think how psychopaths might be useful in these professions.

Can you imagine yourself as a surgeon? I know that the moment I had made my first incision I would be horrified at the blood, the responsibility, the consequence of the patient dying. In other words, I would be a nervous wreck and totally useless. Having someone with a calm detachment, a lack of fear, risk-taking behaviour and no remorse might be the perfect combination for a job that requires 'clinical detachment' from the emotionally charged environment of an operation.

The same would apply to a salesperson selling a product they suspected would not benefit the customer, or a lawyer defending someone accused of a truly heinous act.

So, psychopaths and sociopaths are not completely without merit. They have their uses. But they can be extremely damaging to those around them.

The Luck Of The Psychopath

One of the more fascinating elements of psychopathic behaviour is that they often appear very lucky. But here luck should not be seen as a 'supernatural force'. The luck of the psychopath may be attributed to their ability to pick up the smallest of signals, and changes in mood, atmosphere and circumstance, before others notice the same.

Imagine an office scenario in which the psychopath has been operating. The psychopath may have been manipulating people and circumstance to orchestrate a good outcome for themselves. This may have involved some backstabbing, rumour-spreading, lying or even reputation-destroying behaviour. This may have gone largely unnoticed, and the team appeared to be operating well. But gradually the psychopath's behaviour was beginning to cause the team to unravel and the consequences of this negative behaviour soon to be revealed.

Psychopaths are very good at picking up when the direction of the wind has changed. They normally notice this before others and are therefore able to make their escape before everything goes pear-shaped.

Now here is the strange thing.

Imagine a team where everything seems to have been going well.

Then a key person (the psychopath) leaves the team.

Soon after this person leaves, everything collapses and the consequences of the psychopath's behaviour become evident.

What conclusion might be drawn?

People not involved in the team may not have been aware of, or exposed to, the psychopath's behaviour. They may not have realised the person who left was a psychopath.

It is possible, or even likely, that people both outside and inside the team might conclude the team's collapse happened not because of the psychopath but because the psychopath left the team. In other words, the psychopath was holding it all together.

And people start to miss the psychopath who, meanwhile, has moved on to work their magic in another, possibly higher, team.

How Do You Manage A Relationship With A Psychopath Or Sociopath?

Since neither therapy nor medication can help, there are only three options available to you.

Option 1:

You accept the situation as it is and allow the psychopath or sociopath to do their worst.

This is, of course, a risky strategy. Remember the characteristics of a psychopath are that they have no guilt, no empathy and nothing is ever their fault.

In a relationship with a psychopath one might expect to encounter chronic "gaslighting".

The term "gaslighting" originates from a 1938 play titled "Gaslight" by Patrick Hamilton[4] . In the play, the husband manipulates his wife into believing she's going insane by dimming the gaslights in their house and then insisting to her that they are not dimmed, causing her to doubt

---

4. Gas Light, Patrick Hamilton, Samuel French Limited

her own perceptions and sanity. This concept has since been adapted into psychology to describe a form of emotional abuse where one person manipulates another into questioning their own reality, memory, or sanity. Gaslighting in a working relationship with a psychopathic colleague, employee or boss can manifest in various ways. Here are some examples:

Denying Or Minimising:

Your colleague, employee or boss may deny things they said or did, making you question your memory or perception.

They might downplay the severity of their actions, making you feel like you're overreacting or being too sensitive.

Blaming And Shifting Responsibility:

They may blame you for mistakes or problems that are their fault, causing you to doubt your competence.

They might shift responsibility for their own actions onto you, making you feel guilty or ashamed.

Twisting The Truth:

Your partner, friend, colleague, employee or boss may distort facts or manipulate information to suit their agenda, making it hard for you to trust your own judgement.

They might selectively omit information or cherry-pick data to make themselves look better or to undermine your credibility.

Isolating And Undermining:

They may undermine your relationships with other colleagues or superiors, making you feel isolated and dependent on them for support.

They might spread rumours or gossip about you to damage your reputation and credibility.

In personal relationships they may instigate conflicts with your friends or family and force you to choose between the two. You will, of course, choose the psychopath. This will often result in your being separated and isolated from your normal support network of friends and family.

Projecting Their Insecurities Onto You:

They may accuse you of behaviours or motives that are characteristic of their own behaviour, making you doubt yourself and your intentions.

They might criticise your work or performance in areas where they themselves are lacking, projecting their own insecurities onto you.

In personal relationships your friends or partners may criticise you for the very things they fail themselves. They may tell you that you cannot do a job, a hobby, a skill whilst hiding the real motive that it is a skill, job or hobby that they doubt they could do themselves. Since they don't have the confidence to attempt it they would rather stop you from attempting to be successful in that area.

Manipulating Emotions:

Your colleague, employee or boss may use emotional manipulation tactics such as guilt-tripping or playing the victim to control your behaviour and reactions.

They might use flattery or charm to manipulate you into doing their bidding or to keep you in a state of dependency.

In personal situations the other person may use guilt or emotional blackmail to control you.

They may dismiss your concerns, feelings, or experiences as unimportant or irrelevant, making you doubt the validity of your own emotions.

They might mock or ridicule your emotions or reactions, making you feel ashamed or embarrassed for expressing yourself.

Overall, gaslighting in a working relationship with a psychopathic colleague, employee or boss is aimed at exerting power and control over you, undermining your confidence and autonomy, and manipulating you into compliance or submission.

In personal relationships with a psychopathic or sociopathic partner, family member, or friend, gaslighting can be particularly insidious and damaging.

If you choose Option 1 i.e. 'You accept the situation as it is and allow the psychopath or sociopath to do their worst' you need to be aware of the above. Once in a relationship with a psychopath or sociopath there are no risk-free options. But the option of staying in the relationship may be the riskiest of all.

Option 2:

Hope and pray the psychopath gets bored with you and moves on to another target.

This option also has its risks.

Risk Of Continued Harm:

Psychopaths can be manipulative, charming, and skilled at maintaining control over their targets. They may not easily let go of someone they see as a valuable source of manipulation, gratification, or entertainment. Waiting for them to leave may subject you to continued emotional, psychological, or even physical harm.

Escalation Of Abuse:

Rather than leaving quietly, psychopaths might escalate their abusive tactics if they feel their control slipping or if they sense resistance from their target. This could result in intensified gaslighting, manipulation, or even violent behaviour.

Impact On Mental Health:

Continuing to endure a relationship with a psychopath can have severe detrimental effects on your mental health, including increased anxiety, depression, low self-esteem, and trauma. Waiting for them to leave does not address these issues and can prolong your suffering.

Safety Concerns:

Psychopaths may not simply move on to another target without repercussions. There's a risk that they may stalk, harass, or even harm you if they perceive you as a threat to their control or if they feel rejected.

In summary, waiting and hoping for a psychopath to move may not be a viable or safe solution. It's crucial to prioritise your safety, well-being, and empowerment.

Empowerment Through Action

Rather than passively waiting for the psychopath to leave, taking proactive steps to end the relationship and protect yourself is essential. This may involve seeking support from trusted friends, family, or professionals, developing a safety plan, and setting boundaries to enforce your autonomy and well-being.

This leads to:

Option 3:

Find ways to end the relationship.

Assessing whether to end a business or personal relationship with a psychopath or sociopath requires careful consideration of various factors. Here are steps to help you make an informed decision:

Evaluate The Dynamics:

Reflect on the dynamics of the relationship. Consider whether the relationship is characterised by manipulation, deceit, exploitation, or abuse. Assess how the relationship affects your emotional, psychological, and physical well-being.

Recognise Patterns:

Look for patterns of behaviour exhibited by the individual. Are there consistent signs of manipulation, gaslighting, or disregard for your feelings and boundaries? Pay attention to any red flags or warning signs that indicate the relationship is harmful.

Assess Impact On Your Life:

Consider how the relationship impacts various aspects of your life, including your mental health, self-esteem, personal goals, and professional aspirations. Evaluate whether the relationship enriches or detracts from your overall quality of life.

Seek External Perspectives:

Seek feedback and support from trusted friends, family members, or professionals who can provide objective perspectives on the situation. Their insights can help you gain clarity and perspective on the dynamics of the relationship. You may be afraid to do this since it is likely you have become isolated from these people for a time. You may have been encouraged by the psychopath to have a fight or argument with these people, ensuring the end of the relationship. When you are considering leaving the psychopath, you might be nervous about approaching old friends or family. Consider, however, that if these people ever loved you, they will have been hurt to lose you. Some of them may have been very aware that you were under the influence of the psychopath and will be delighted you are finally making the attempt to break free.

Establish Boundaries:

If you decide to maintain the relationship, establish clear and firm boundaries to protect yourself from manipulation, exploitation, or abuse. Communicate your boundaries assertively and be prepared to enforce them if they are violated.

Consider Potential Risks:

Before you do anything, assess the potential risks of ending the relationship, such as retaliation, harassment, or attempts to undermine your reputation or livelihood. Develop a safety plan to mitigate these risks and ensure your well-being. This is paramount. It is easy to say but harder to do. There is no risk-free option in a relationship of this type. Sadly, doing nothing, also carries a risk. But, **before you take any option or decision,** take whatever steps you can to ensure the physical and mental safety of yourself and any affected dependents e.g. children.

Prioritise Self-Care:

Prioritise self-care and well-being throughout the decision-making process. Engage in activities that promote your physical, emotional, and psychological health, such as exercise, therapy, meditation, or spending time with supportive individuals.

Trust Your Instincts:

Trust your instincts and intuition when making the decision. If something feels off or if you sense that the relationship is harmful, prioritise your instincts and take steps to protect yourself.

Ultimately, the decision to end a relationship with a psychopath or sociopath should be based on your own well-being, safety, and empowerment. If the relationship is causing significant harm or if you feel unable to establish healthy boundaries, ending the relationship may be the best option for your long-term health and happiness.

Chapter 19
Conclusion

As we draw the curtain on our exploration of dealing with difficult people, let's take a moment to reflect on the key messages and strategies that have guided us through this intricate terrain.

Throughout this journey, we've emphasised the importance of understanding the basics of dealing with difficult people. Central to this understanding is the ability to empathetically perceive the other person's "map of the world" – their unique perspectives, motivations, and emotional states. By recognising and respecting these differences, we lay the groundwork for effective communication and conflict resolution. Remember "To be understood, first seek to understand"

Assertiveness emerges as a fundamental skill in our arsenal for navigating challenging interactions. Through assertive communication, we assert our needs and boundaries with clarity and confidence, fostering mutual respect and understanding. The use of "I" messages empowers us to express our feelings and perspectives without assigning blame, paving the way for constructive dialogue and problem-solving.

Moreover, we've delved into the intricate workings of paradigms and heuristics, understanding how these cognitive frameworks shape our perceptions and interactions. By challenging our own biases and assumptions, we expand our capacity for empathy and open-mindedness, fostering deeper connections with those around us.

Active listening and the art of asking good quality open-ended and probing questions emerge as powerful tools for building rapport and resolving conflicts. Through attentive listening and thoughtful enquiry, we demonstrate genuine interest and empathy, creating space for authentic dialogue and mutual understanding.

In addition to these foundational principles, we've explored specific strategies for dealing with a variety of challenging personalities. From Bullies and Dominators to Jeering Jesters, Scornful Snipers, Double-Dealing Deceivers, Moaning Monsters, Silent But Deadly and even psychopaths and sociopaths, we've equipped ourselves with a diverse toolkit for broadening our options when dealing with a wide range of difficult behaviours.

One final note is to remember that the journey of dealing with difficult people is not merely about overcoming obstacles, but about embracing opportunities for growth and connection. We often dread dealing with difficult people and situations and most of us would rather avoid them if possible. We see them as some of our darkest moments and it can be hard to approach them with anything but fear and trepidation. There is, however, a more positive side to consider. It is both possible and likely that your deepest fears may not be realised. You may find that addressing the difficult situation doesn't mean the end of the relationship or even just the end of the bad behaviour. Instead, you may find that addressing the difficult situation leads to an improvement in both the situation and the relationship. There are times in my own life where I have been unhappy with the behaviour of a colleague or personal acquaintance, and I have used many of these techniques to help me. In some of these situations (not all) the result has been an improvement in both the situation and the relationship. In several cases, addressing the situation has helped me to turn someone I once considered an 'enemy' into a long-term dear friend.

I have been asked, "How do you know this stuff will work?"

I can give two answers to that.

Firstly, nothing will work in every situation. Dealing with difficult people requires you to broaden your 'toolkit' so you have as many techniques as possible to give you a wide range of responses. It is your task to choose the right approach for the situation. You will, almost certainly, get it wrong sometimes. The aim of this book is to increase the number of times you get it right.

Secondly, in the interests of 'science' I decided to try an experiment once. I knew all these techniques, but I encountered a situation in my personal life which I would have described as difficult, and hurtful. Since I knew the situation could not affect my professional life, I decided to abandon all the techniques in this book and just give full unrestrained access to my emotions. I did what came 'naturally' and let my anger and frustration pour out. I am still living with the consequences of that decision over eight years later. As an experiment, it was worth it to strengthen my belief that the techniques described in this book do increase the likelihood of reaching a more satisfactory outcome for you and the other person. But would I do such an experiment again? No, I would not.

By approaching challenging interactions with empathy, assertiveness, and an open heart, I believe we cultivate deeper insights into ourselves and others, fostering richer, more fulfilling relationships in all aspects of our lives.

May the tips and techniques and strategies outlined in these pages help you on your continued journey towards greater understanding, empathy, and connection as they have, undoubtedly, helped me.

Geoff Marsh

Manufactured by Amazon.ca
Bolton, ON

39628735R00122